The Music of Chopin and the Rule of St Benedict

Bernard Sawicki OSB

The Music of Chopin and the Rule of St Benedict

A Mystical Panorama of Life

Bibliographic Information published by the Deutsche Nationalbibliothek
The Deutsche Nationalbibliothek lists this publication
in the Deutsche Nationalbibliografie; detailed bibliographic
data is available in the internet at http://dnb.d-nb.de.

Library of Congress Cataloging-in-Publication Data
Sawicki, Bernard.
 [Muzyka Chopina a Regula sw. Benedykta. English]
 The music of Chopin and the Rule of St Benedict : a mystical panorama of life/ Bernard Sawicki OSB ; translation into English, Zofia Weaver.
   pages cm
 Includes index.
 ISBN 978-3-631-65065-3
 1. Chopin, Frédéric, 1810-1849—Criticism and interpretation. 2. Benedict, Saint, Abbot of Monte Cassino. Regula—Influence. I. Weaver, Zofia, 1947- II. Title.
 ML410.C54S2513 2014
 786.2092—dc23
                                                                    2014019167

Translation into English: Zofia Weaver

Cover image: Simon Stubbs OSB

This publication was financially supported
by Elizabeth Shirzad.

ISBN 978-3-631-65065-3 (Print)
E-ISBN 978-3-653-04190-3 (E-Book)
DOI 10.3726/978-3-653-04190-3

© Peter Lang GmbH
Internationaler Verlag der Wissenschaften
Frankfurt am Main 2014
All rights reserved.
Peter Lang Edition is an Imprint of Peter Lang GmbH.
Peter Lang – Frankfurt am Main · Bern · Bruxelles · New York ·
Oxford · Warszawa · Wien
All parts of this publication are protected by copyright.
Any utilisation outside the strict limits of the copyright law, without
the permission of the publisher, is forbidden and liable to prosecution.
This applies in particular to reproductions, translations, microfilming,
and storage and processing in electronic retrieval systems.

This publication has been peer reviewed.

www.peterlang.com

For my fellow Brethren

MOTTO: Do you know that reading music in silence and listening to it in the imagination is perfect joy? Yes, when I cannot leave my bed, and this happens often, I get them to bring me not the works of the Church Fathers, but sheet music. (...) And what do you think I ask for...? No, not Bach at all, not even Mozart ... Chopin. (...) This is the purest music of all...
 Bonifacio Krug, Abbot of Monte Cassino, to André Gide[1]

---

[1] Quoted after the Polish translation of A. Gide's *Notatki o Chopinie*, transl. M. Musiał, Kraków 2007, pp. 13–14.

Contents

Introduction	11
The Background and the Presuppositions	13
Defining the Area of Similarities	21
The Risk of Beginning	29
Beginnings and Trust	35
Authority	43
Weakness	49
Interactions and Relationships	55
The Others – Patience and Consistency	65
The Yearning	73
Emotions	79
The Details	87
The Melody – A Treatise on Embodied Grace	97
How to end?	107
The Coda: on the Waves of the World – A Meditation on Benedictine life today	117
PS: The Aporias of Chopin's music – The *Rule* is Only the Beginning	123
A Hypothetical Ending: On the Other Side	135
Index of Works by Fryderyk Chopin Referrred to in the Text	141
Index	143

Introduction

The inspiration for this work came from many sources. It is still a somewhat sketchy draft of an idea which is impossible to express fully and clearly. Perhaps this is what happens to every very personal reflection which has been in the making for too long and at too deep a level.

Yet, when trying to share the most personal, and often surprising, discoveries, we can only test them by trying to "objectivise" them in various ways. The circumstances in which this takes place either encourage one to be bolder and continue the search, or destroy one's illusions without mercy. The idea of juxtaposing the music of Chopin with the *Rule* of St Benedict formed the basis of the Retreat I gave to two Benedictine communities in Canada: the convent of Sainte-Marie des Deux-Montagnes and the abbey of Saint-Benoît-du-Lac. The favourable reaction there encouraged me to develop my thoughts into a "Mystical Chopin" project, a contribution by the Abbey of Tyniec to the celebration of the 200th anniversary of Fryderyk Chopin's birth. The reflections which came about in this way offer a wide range of reasons for linking Chopin's music with the Benedictine tradition in general, and with the Abbey of Tyniec in particular. However, there is a difficulty in presenting this material in full since, naturally, Chopin's music has to be an integral part of it. This means that, where necessary, music quotations need to be skilfully merged with the verbal discourse. Thus, technically, the following procedures have been adopted: a) shorter fragments, to which the text refers directly, are given in music notation in the text; b) when talking about whole works, the full title of a given composition appears in brackets, preceded by an asterisk (*); this is an invitation to listen to the music in whatever performance is preferred or available; c) at the end of the text there is a full list of Chopin's compositions to which the text refers. Those which need to be heard in full while reading the text are marked with an asterisk (*). The ideal solution would be a multimedia text with an integrated audio recording, and perhaps this will one day be possible. In the meantime, we adhere to the traditional book form, but one that is open to interaction with a music recording.

Editing the consecutive parts of this essay made it increasingly clear that what is recorded here are only glimpses, or traces, of a much larger reality which, in somewhat grandiose terms, might be described as theology of music; one, however, that can only be discovered in its pure flow alone, without reference to text or to extra-musical reality. It would thus be an "implicit" theology of pure musical flow in itself. The possibility of such a theology is one of the main questions which this text indirectly tries to answer. It seems, however, that it might be possible to develop the themes presented here. How this is to happen remains an open and tempting prospect, which allows one to treat this discourse with some forbearance, as an embryo of a larger discourse which might, one day, be developed and systematised. But before this happens, it would be useful for this text to be tested further, and the readers' reception of it would undoubtedly provide such a test. Naturally, this means making the idea accessible in this publication. The nature of the subject makes it difficult to foresee who will be the readers of this discourse. Perhaps it will find its way to many, perhaps to just a few. Whatever its fate, this is an attempt to look in a different way both at the music of Chopin, and the *Rule* of St Benedict. If this helps anyone, so much the better: it will mean that it was worthwhile to give it a permanent form.

The Background and the Presuppositions

The existence of the concept of analogy, or perhaps one should say the necessity for its existence, is as obvious as it is mysterious. We look for connections and for kinships, we search for them and find them in the most diverse areas of our life. Not only our imagination, but all our thinking draws on them. In a sense, everything is possible here. One might say that, the more original or improbable the link or the connection, the better. At the same time, however, we examine closely and carefully the principles on which such constructions are built. This is always an opportunity for, and an example of, the greatness and transcendence of human thought, or perhaps even the expression of the longing, deep in our hearts, for encompassing the reality in which we live all at once, a desire for some universal synthesis.[2] This longing was very close to the heart of Romanticism. We accept wholeheartedly the claim made by Przybylski, that "during the Romantic period, when music was believed to be the proto-principle of being, musical metaphors were particularly favoured."[3]

Thus, it is possible that Chopin's music is in some way related to the *Rule* of St Benedict.

It is a justifiable kinship, as are many others. Perceiving it, or just indicating its possibility, offers a point of departure for our deliberations. But this is only the beginning. One should justify such a suggestion, and then test it as fully as possible. This would involve not so much trying to make an argument for the "Benedictine" character of Chopin's music, however one might understand it; rather, we need to demonstrate the similarities and convergences between these two creations of the human spirit, so different and yet so manifestly outstanding.

Even though one's awareness of a kinship between the *Rule* of St Benedict and Chopin's music may be tentative and not explicit, it clearly presents a problem of approach and presentation. How is one to place alongside each other two worlds which speak a different language and function in totally different areas of human culture?

Chopin – well, we all know: an overwhelming essence of Polishness, amazingly universal at the same time, yet always so much ours and ... so human,

---

[2] The issue of the metaphysical and theological character of analogy, which is key to these deliberations and which will be presented indirectly, is discussed by Erich Przywara in his *Analogia entis*, Freiburg 1996[III], a classic in this area.

[3] R. Przybylski, *Cień jaskółki. Esej o myślach Chopina*, Kraków 1995, p. 265.

encompassing all the registers of existence that is the human fate, yet fixed in a particular time and place, and rooted in a specific culture and territory – in this case, that of Poland.

Universality, expressed and realised through that which is particular – that is the common platform of Chopin's music and the message of St Benedict– the charismatic embodiment of the universal message of the Church. The unity and harmony of the world manifests itself in the multiplicity of particular forms, aspects, beings and relationships. How does this happen? How is this diversity fulfilled in that unity and harmony? The answer to this question not only provides justification for claiming kinship between Chopin's music and St Benedict's *Rule* – it also opens the way to discovering many analogies, sometimes surprising, which allow us to look in a different way at concepts within which we usually operate more or less automatically.

Various areas of reality are organised into certain archetypal structures, whose forms are characterised by some degree of kinship. One can find them on a variety of levels; they are the foundation of human activity: poetry, philosophy, mysticism. They grow out of analogy, and their nature might be described as "modular" – a concept we shall return to later. Let us take as our point of departure the idea that talking about the kinship between diverse areas of reality which seem very distant from each other is possible because of clearly defined and graspable parameters. That is because every part of reality with a clearly defined identity is a microcosm of some kind, constructed according to a particular logic and ruled by its own laws. This logic and these rules are the platform on which kinships can be found, and these exist between parts capable of being separated out, segments of complex realities in a relationship of analogy or kinship to each other. It is these segments which we will regard as "modules". Each of them is something of a microcosm, a landscape and a story in itself, and one can try to distinguish the components of each one. Each module would thus be a variation on the theme of these elements, or, rather, a symphony composed of these elements. What is most fascinating is the coincident, not to say complementary, nature of these modules. We feel – at least we intuit – the possibility of their mutual translation. After all, they all describe how human beings fit into the natural existential contexts.

What is the character of these modules? Are they an ideal construction or a set of desiderata? Or perhaps they are a record of experience, of life on the horizon of transcendence, our encounter with "the other", as well as our being suspended between heaven and earth, good and evil? And thus one creates a landscape of relationships, both those fulfilled and embryonic, but above all faithful to the human experience of yearning and fulfilment, expectation and satisfaction. This solidarity with human fate tempts one to regard such landscapes more as a haven and a hiding place than a sign of a road being travelled. Or is it, perhaps, a suggestion, an invitation to share some kind of experience?

This, then, is one way of looking both at the world of the *Rule* of St Benedict and the spaces of Chopin's music. Both realities, clear and intricate in their construction, are, indeed, a record of life experience and an open invitation to participate. Both demand effort, one might even say – initiation. But both fascinate, leaving one in awe of their breadth and vision, as well as their closeness to humankind. Both, each in its own way, enchant and enrapture, and so there is nothing strange in their paths becoming more entwined in the area of perception and reception. Both the text of St Benedict's *Rule* and the notation of Chopin's compositions have a purpose and serve to indicate something; they demand to come alive, to be made concrete. They are open forms, awaiting content; a potential which expects to be realised. That is what their universality implies – and, paradoxically, it can only be captured by acquiring detail, like a drama which demands very specific staging. Both realities are thus a medium, an indication and a guide to possibilities which, when realised, create a tradition, the Benedictine and the Chopinian one. The world of the legacy of the creator – the rule-giver or the composer – is a record based on clearly defined principles, as well as a projection of certain principles. However, it demands interaction, a dialogue with someone who will want to interpret it and act on it. In practice, this means an encounter with a concrete person. One might say, this is a "giving of oneself" to another, to other people, to the future generations, with all the limitations and delicacy that this entails. Here there must be contact, mutual acceptance and understanding, a resonance of various sensibilities and experiences. It is in this sense that both the *Rule* and the musical text are a medium, a form demanding content, lines asking to be coloured, a palette offered to colour a diversity of landscapes.

Each such mediation is thus, on the one hand, a condition of a given text coming alive and, on the other, a point of departure for new creative and expressive qualities coming into being. It is also a manifestation of our mutual dependence. For new content to be created, for it to be passed on, we must occupy spaces which someone had arranged earlier, and we may use tools which someone had invented before us. If such an interaction takes place, if a given text, a legacy, lives on and resonates with the recipients,that is its test – a sign that it concerns not just its author. It goes beyond being purely private and becomes a shared value; it is no longer an individual matter, linked to a definite time and place. The author then is no longer of the greatest importance, but, rather, becomes a servant in the creation of new perspectives, new content and new relationships. The experience which bore fruit in a given text begins to radiate, flowing out in ever wider circles, no longer belonging just to its creator. In this way the actions of an artist (composer) and a saint come together, taking on, in a sense, a priestly character. Indeed, both work for a cause which is greater than they are, and is not their personal idea. Both open worlds which they are not capable of fully encompassing or comprehending, fully inhabiting or populating. They can only be the doormen, the caretakers, the guides. And so, sooner or later, they feel the necessity of distancing themselves, in order to make room for us to embody and fill out the shapes which it was in their gift to create; for us to admire and populate the world which they created.

Indirectly, this points to the existence of a supra-earthly inspiration – obvious, naturally, in the case of a saint, but not necessarily an unfounded claim in the case of an artist. Indeed, in both cases the usual course of earthly affairs is interrupted, ordinary logic and practice are suspended. This intrigues and attracts so much as to give an impression of bearing traces of being not of this world. If we look at the artist and the saint from such a perspective, they both seem to be working towards the same goal – as if "preparing the way for the Lord" (Mark 3,1; Luke 1,76) – discreetly, sensitively, but unmistakably so.

A text – and this applies to the *Rule* as well as a musical composition – is undoubtedly a record of a life, the markings of a road travelled and struggles undergone. All this only testifies to its authenticity, honesty, and integrity. The creation of a convincing and attractive micro-cosmos testifies to its deeply human authenticity, and to the value of searching for the meaning of life. It points in the right direction, towards something more than oneself.

In the microcosm of life, reflected in the universe of a created work, points of intersection of ideals, dreams, possibilities, intuitions and efforts to realise them, all come together. All of them are directed along the line of a person's experience of the human existential condition. That is why we can treat them in a modular fashion and find ourselves in them; this, in turn, makes it possible to develop analogies and to discover kinships, to juxtapose diverse elements from realities seemingly distant from each other. Thus, taking delight in the abundance of aspects of human activity, we may, in a sense, fit its fruits to our own sensitivities, culture, or needs. It is always possible to change one's perspective, to go back or forward, to take a look from another angle.

Every world has its own constituents, but each also corresponds to general categories which make it possible to describe other worlds. It is both a human creation and a human environment, testifying to man's relationship to himself, to others and to Transcendence, as a result of the interweaving relationships which bind us to the environment in which we live. As a whole it is orderly. It is ruled by a logic which results from the projection of the inner world of the individual and his interaction with the external environment. The axes are the directions of our relationships, characterised by varying shades and varying intensity. On that basis there arise a superstructure of specific complexes of states – emotional, volitional or cognitive – and the most diverse forms of bonds to the environment, which in practice create a network of our functioning in the world. The key concept here is that of shape, of *Gestalt* – the *Gestalt psychology* approach, and the theology of Hans Urs von Balthasar.[4] Shape understood in this way is a marker and a unit of meaning, defining the whole and referring the meaning of fragments to it. Shape is what focuses attention, and makes concentration and contemplation possible. Through details and their mutual interplay, it enables us to enter the depth of the relationships within the network of the total reality constituted from various parts. The shape and the details which create it and define it combine into larger sets and systems which form still higher levels of meaning or discourse, thus revealing even more suggestively the richness of the relationships which already exist. Shape understood in this way is the essence of the module referred to earlier. It allows us to distinguish and identify it: the shape, the points, the lines and the places where a given world possibly encounters other worlds, or perhaps just the traces of their interactions. All this, of course, is a result of our existential condition. However, these modules make it possible to freeze in time – in memory or in imagination – that which is momentary, unimaginable and fleeting; the mysterious expression of that *more* which marks out the final direction and the meaning of our existence. It is both the point of departure and the material for symbols or metaphors, the appropriate tissue for analogies, and thus both for metaphysics and poetry. It is, lastly, a carrier of human communication and the condition of existence of different styles of being in the world, and understanding the world.

To make thinking in terms of modules accessible in a different way, one might use the image of the world's "structure" being, in a sense, granular (however we might understand the term). It is made up of threads, of strands – like a cosmos made up of individual nebulae and galaxies. It is these bundles of meanings and contents, the little clods of them, which we are trying to define as modules. States of the spirit, volitional states, combine here with various shades of human interrelationships, as well as man's relationship with the world and, above all, with

---

4 Cf.H.U. von Balthasar, *Herrlichkeit. Eine theologische Ästhetik*, Bd I. *Schau der Gestalt*, Einsiedeln 1973. Here the word *shape* seems most appropriate, especially in relation to musical reality; we shall use it, but with the meaning ascribed to it by H.U. von Balthasar.

Transcendence. There is an infinity of such modules, but they can be captured. They allow one to order and encompass the boundlessness of the whole of reality. This is because they are, in a sense, bundles of simple, one-sided categories which in practice we use as the most common attributes – sad, happy, lazy, heavy, bright, transparent etc. Like chemical compounds and their molecules, they come together in a variety of combinations, creating new qualities, sufficiently discernible to undertake an attempt to describe them by developing an appropriate discourse. There may be many such descriptions, and they can be organised in different ways, so that discourses can arise which are dependent on the sequence and order of the description.

What do we achieve by the use of such modules and their descriptions? It allows us to search, blindly and timidly but with a degree of hope, for rules and kinships existing between different areas of reality. In this way we can come to know, and even meditate on, the path to shaping and developing various relationships, including the striving towards Transcendence, taken by others. We can thus perceive an aspect of Mystery revealed in this way, Mystery made tangible through contact or relationship with what is tangible. Through this, we ourselves may be moved and enraptured by the closeness and accessibility of Transcendence.

We can thus talk about such modules as: the beginning; passion; longing; but also delicate sadness; timid heroism; perseverance in striving forward in spite of obstacles; gentleness; compassion for another's weakness; resoluteness; zest. Such modules may be (and are) constituted by characters in books or films, their stories and encounters. And yes, whole poems, novels, pictures, works of art, scenes are also, in a sense, modules. A module is a distinctive, newly perceptible quality which we cannot ignore. It intrigues us and forces us to take note of it, opening up to us and at the same time directing us to somewhere further on. There will never be fulfilment in it – more likely a yearning. That is how the space of our encounters – with other people, with the world, with Transcendence – is created. That is how the space of creative progress in our life is created, its stages of development and its growing depth.

Modules combine in a variety of ways – mainly through the threads they share, which also determine the kinship between them. Various modules, or just parts of them, may combine in configurations which create new, separately integral qualities, series of meanings and events which are complementary to the whole universe of the particular set of modules. In this way we get strands of shades and colours carrying particular content or emotions – units that are not only expressive but existential, leading motifs of a given world, but at the same time a dimension which goes beyond that world and makes it possible to relate it to other worlds. This is a tangible expression of the unity and similarity of human strivings, evidence for the existence of a common foundation, source and goal of diverse human paths. In this way, through the stories of human hearts and generations – but also through art and history – run the lines and threads of prayer, idyll, struggle, elegance, rejection, creation, building and destroying: the paths of individuals and of communities, exaltation and despair.

It is just such modular perception of both the *Rule* of St Benedict and of Chopin's music which allows us (but does not oblige us) to see their kinship – if only on the basis of the example of reconciliation and mutual explanation through different worlds. Let us therefore take a look at the planes which mark out these kinships.

It means, primarily, measuring up to the highest ideals that are difficult to realise, although in both cases they are quite clearly delineated. Everything happens in the context of an awareness of human frailty, expressed equally sincerely and unpretentiously by the music of Chopin (with all the changeability of its moods, fragility, melancholy and distress over an irrevocable past), and by the *Rule* of St Benedict (tirelessly proclaiming the same respect for the human measure, limits and possibilities). Both approaches give us a description of mankind – both analytic and synthetic – that is throughout true, positive, powerful and strongly drawn.

Another matter is the nature of the charisma both of the Benedictine order and of Chopin's music: at the meeting point, that which is Polish combines with a universal wisdom, and this happens through simplicity, liveliness and dignity, at the same time opening up to emotion and sensitivity; not without heroism and days of greatness – as well as disasters. A symbol of this, which can be interpreted as a seal legitimising the suggested kinship, is Tyniec Abbey – a Benedictine monastery that has grown into a landscape so very Polish, both geographically (the Vistula, the weeping willows, the meadows, the picturesque hills, the little rocks) and historically (the old walls, the ruined towers, a testimony to the glory and drama of the history of our homeland). It is not only the silhouette of the church that complements the ordinary, rustic landscape – the very buildings of Tyniec are rustic; although very few original wooden cottages are left today, the rhythms, the defiance and the flair of the oldest surviving buildings are Polish to the core – as if listening out, waiting to join in the lofty note sounded by religion, the chorale and the gentry. Such a synthesis of the peasant Poland is most typical for Chopin and for Tyniec – with the full spectrum of the hidden, sun-drenched pain and extraordinarily lively vigour, as well as the bitterness of nostalgia for the past that is irrevocably lost, and the desire that it should not disappear, at least as a point of reference.

This is also the case with regard to the style, clearly defined and perceptible both in the text of the *Rule* and in Chopin's music. It is closely bound with the message of the content, with its spirit, but remains subordinate to it. Here, moderation and restraint harmoniously accompany existential authenticity and deep emotionality. Paradoxically, they serve to highlight the expression rather than limit it, and the expression itself attracts with the richness and authenticity of experience, with simplicity and sincerity; we find in it all that is the most human, and thus the most moving, but it is ennobled, aspiring to that which is the most elevated and heavenly. In this sense, the music of Chopin appears not only as a picture of a life, but also as one of many intermediaries between the message of the Benedictine *Rule* and life. The various commentaries to the *Rule*, or attempts to interpret it, are also forms of such mediation. The reality of human condition, as well as the fragility and beauty of human existence, expressed through the lines and gestures of Chopin's music, fit perfectly into the ideal drawn by St Benedict. Chopin himself, with all his enormous sense of creative responsibility, never had great aspirations. Consciously limiting himself to only one means of expression, i.e., the piano, he still achieved so much. St Benedict's *Rule* was also never an expression of excessive ambition. Its author emphasised that it was only the "least" Rule, a humble path "written for a beginning" (73, 9)[5]. In view of this, both these realities occupy the same level – in a sense, both equally helpless. This, perhaps, is the final, quiet but particularly convincing argument for the existence of a kinship between the music of Chopin and the *Rule* of St Benedict.

---

[5] I am grateful to St Benedict's Abbey in Atchison, Kansas, for their kind permission to use the English translation of *The Holy Rule of Saint Benedict* by Fr. Boniface Verheyen, available at their website, http://rule.kansasmonks.org. Later quotations follow this edition (RulBen); the first number is the chapter number, the second the verse number.

Defining the Area of Similarities

Talking about the most important things carries with it the danger of saying too much. In a sense, this is a necessary evil, of which one needs to constantly remind oneself. This concerns both spiritual matters, and music. Talking about the "inexpressible" is a perpetual temptation and, at the same time, an experience of helplessness. Yet, perhaps, this makes it authentically human, and thus close to our hearts and needs? In this, our main experience is that of humility which, like a golden thread, links all our authentic and sincere strivings, and these become more effective as new questions arise, abundantly emerging from that "little" that we have succeeded in knowing. It is a profound truth about humankind's existential situation and destiny that we are forever seeking without being satisfied. This corresponds to the mood of St Augustine's *Confessions* as well as St Benedict's advice on making sure that one "really seeketh God"[6].

From that space emerge all kinds of possible kinships between the diverse threads of reality. It is both a space of synthesis and encounter. They seek each other and realise themselves most fully in symbols, that is, in areas which have their own specific laws, although they are open to all kinds of connections. Symbols are like the nodes in a network of modules. In them our relationships focus and cross, and different worlds are mutually explained. Our deliberations will follow that trail of symbols. A line of associations marked out in this way will also turn out to be a clear axis of kinship.

Returning to the encounter between the music of Chopin and St Benedict's *Rule*, we come back to the image of Tyniec Abbey. It can be seen as a form of synthesis which combines, in a way that is both classical and archetypal, that which is Polish with that which is religious. This is a possible foundation of the kinship we are talking about.

This synthesis takes place primarily in the historical dimension. That dimension, however, is understood in an untypical manner – paradoxically, it is open to the generally functioning stereotypes, as well as the whole Romantic legacy understood in the widest sense. It is thus a history rooted in the Middle Ages – those legendary, mysterious times where we find the world of noble knights and their deeds, their battles and their loves, a world of bygone glory, with its reflections and splinters. These are not just reminiscences, but a living reality which can and

---

6   RulBen 58,8.

should be entered in search of one's identity. It is dominated by severity and simplicity – but also by bold gestures, a pensive restraint, without chiaroscuro or retouching, a history painstakingly carved in time as if in stone. Here the contrasts which demand a larger space and greater importance function all the more profoundly.

This is the character of Chopin's *Ballade No. 1 in G minor* op. 23, which seems to emerge from the vapours of the past, operating with a severe melodic line, and – if softened with a pastel contrast – it is only to emphasise this severity. Bold gestures and restraint of the material used are the main dimensions of the style that dominates here.

That medieval – one might perhaps say "proto-Polish" – world of values and past glories is so suggestive that it cannot be reduced to being a memory. Its form and content are brought into the present by their values – old yet still valid. It is a world so familiar from our childhood, which we always look back to with longing. In it, the loftiest ideals were so very important and so real that one was ready to do anything not to lose sight of them. Our thoughts were always returning to them, they coloured our encounters with people and the games we played. Who was not fascinated by the little lead or plastic soldiers, both sappers and hussars? Who did not glue together models of planes or ships? What girl was not absorbed in playing with her dolls? And there were the books, the plays, the films, crowded with – knights of course, but also kings, princes and princesses. These are the reveries, the dreams of our childhood which remain with us, somewhere deep in our hearts, forever. (*Ballade No. 1 in G minor* op. 23)[7]

Whether we like it or not, such longing for bygone times is very much present in the Benedictine tradition, particularly in its most recent version, which, to a large extent, attempts to consciously recreate the models of a distant past, usually interpreted in a highly idealistical and romantic manner. This is the style which dominates the architecture, but also the customs and even the habits worn in monasteries restored during the last two centuries. Yet it is quite natural and appropriate that it should evoke an aura of mysteriousness and exoticism, which have always been associated with the world of monasteries, particularly the oldest ones and, thus, obviously, the Benedictine ones. These are the meanings one can hear in *Fantasia in F-minor* op. 49 – even more severe and noble, even more full of ideals than *Ballade in G-minor* mentioned a moment ago. There is less narration here, but more etiquette and … ethos. It is a picture of a world which faithfully

---

7   The asterisk (*) indicates the point where it would be helpful to listen to the work being discussed.

follows certain principles, a world sanctified by tradition. Everything here moves with a rhythm established from time immemorial, even the most sincere and most passionate yearnings of the heart are cloaked in moderation. At the same time, it is a world imbued with reflection. Any development, and quickening, are immediately toned down and checked with moments of thoughtfulness. (*Fantasia in F minor op. 49)

We would not keep returning so willingly and constantly to that world of medieval stories and legends if they were only monumental events carved in bronze. That world also has bright colours, and a grace and lightness of its own. We find them in the joyful, lively rusticity, in its idyllic nature, fresh, even if defiant at times. That world combines both nobility and innocence, youth and an ancient call of blood. These are the sounds of folk music, from the heart of which grow Chopin's mazurkas. We feel also here that nature, sun, a village landscape, create a unique and unforgettable aura of a paradise lost yet very tangible; we hear the tones of some primeval and universal harmony that is familiar to everyone and awakens a yearning – a harmony full of life, sun, freshness, dash and verve, so typical of youth. It is worth remembering that a feeling similar to this aura accompanied the first monks, particularly those whose life was rooted in the Celtic tradition[8] , perhaps less so in the case of those dwelling in the Egyptian desert, Syria or Palestine. Much of such an "idyllic" content fills Chopin's early opuses. We find an incomparable, emblematic example of it in *Fantasia on Polish Airs in A major* op.13, full of freshness and light (*Fantasia on Polish Airs in A major* op. 13). A similar note is to be found also in Chopin's later works, such as his *Mazurka in F major* op. 68 No. 3. (*Mazurka in F major* op. 68 No. 3)

Yet the carefree evocation of childhood and its colours is not everything. Both in Chopin's works and in the Benedictine ethos there are areas that are darker and more difficult. Their presence might be described as the shadow and the burden of history, full of the tragedy of wars, uprisings and struggles for liberation. It is such a very Polish struggle for independence and identity. A sense of helplessness is combined there with the spirit of rebellion, valour with the experience of defeat. In some ways like a small child, desperately clenching its fists with tears pouring down its face. But in truth the matter is deadly serious, touching the deepest wounds of our history, and while clearly these wounds are evidence of glory, that glory belongs to the past, or is even lost altogether. Yet it is the description of the struggle, the arduous striving for justice and meaning that come across most

---

8   Its traces can be found in J.H. Newman's essay *The Benedictine Order* published by Wydawnictwo Benedyktynów TYNIEC in 1993, Polish transl. P. Mroczkowski.

strongly. There is much pain and effort here, but always a determination to succeed, since it is all "in the right cause". Perhaps today one should listen to *Etude in C minor* op. 10 No. 12, the "Revolutionary Etude," with that attitude in mind? (*Etude in C minor op. 10 No. 12)

In all this we see our life, or, rather, the monastic life: a remembrance and a return to a lost paradise, a struggle to gain the right and find the path to it; in a word – a continuous, grand recapitulation of humanity on the horizon of faith. Music is its image and its record. It carries in it traces of the yearning, the seeking and the striving, sometimes profoundly moving. The thing is – for the present, we live here and now. Chopin's music, the same now as before, may provide a stable point of reference, an ageless testing ground where we can keep on testing the search and the struggle for that which is most important – including, ultimately, the search for God. If it is true that music is a form of silence (in the words of Lutosławski), then there is all the more need, in this world of uproar and noise, to learn not to lose sight of what is most important, to always look for meaning, constantly and actively listening to, immersing oneself in silence, always finding new movements, motifs and values which pulsate in the depths of silence.

Such a point of view might be accused of too much subjectivity. Can one say anything adequate about music without falling into the trap of banality or exaggeration? A positive answer to this dilemma might be attempted through drawing attention to the fact that the music of Chopin is an amazing form of subjectivism which achieved an objective, universal dimension. The same applies to the Benedictine tradition, with its continuing challenge posed not only for each monk, but for each monastery. This challenge is taken up through the vow of stability, which firmly grounds both the monk and the monastery in a particular place and time. Binding the monk by these conditions, the vows at the same time make him become a part of a single tradition that grows from an intensely personal experience of one man, St Benedict: an individual experience thus raised to the rank of a general norm. This both allows and demands that each Benedictine monastery should always be open to new currents and to visitors, to whom it should transmit the values which lie at the foundations of the Benedictine tradition. Such fidelity of that which is particular to that which is general is a measure of a theology faithful to the Incarnation – one which confesses a solidarity with humankind and with God, expressing the divine through the human. It is through such an approach that the works of Chopin take on a symbolic meaning, becoming an analogy of monastic life, a platform of solidarity. Today, when the world's interest in God grows less, and religion is seen more in the categories of magic than an existential event, one needs to search all the more eagerly for new and fresh forms of expression and witness of authentic human life – sufficiently expressive to be noticed, and to be convincing to the world. Viewed in this light, these deliberations may provide inspiration for improving one's biblical knowledge, or experiencing the liturgy, or even for increasing our sensitivity to the surrounding world.

Chopin's music thus turns out to be a path from the particular to the general, marked out and tested by its faithfulness to shared values, and the possibility of incarnate theology. Chopin appears here as a witness and a prophet, who transmits and expresses these values almost ... like a monk. It is a testimony to the struggle for independence and freedom, to the necessity of commitment, both in order to defend these values, and to illuminate and pass them on, since these are the values that are decisive in determining our identity. It is for them that we lead a life which, from the purely human point of view, appears incomprehensible, or even impossible, in the eyes of the world.

On the other hand, Chopin's music might offer a chance of renewing the knowledge of the *Rule* and, in practical terms, a study of the "monastic" theology, i.e., a theology that is all-embracing, wise and human, that enables the discovery of a mysticism that is close to people: accessible and integrating, always open to exploration as a basis of meditation, as an open view of the world and the experiencing of it; and also as a way, a style of being. It is, in sum, an integrating component, like an artist who feels and sees more, and sometimes succeeds in combining contradictions. Should not such an attitude characterise people who live by a *Rule* which begins with the words: "Listen, O my son, to the precepts of thy master"?

All the above remarks arrange themselves into an expressive landscape which we can garner – or discover – in *Impromptu in G-flat major* op. 51. It is a story, an impression, both absorbing and mysterious, depicting lands of the imagination, multicoloured and nostalgic, those created in the imagination and those that are quite real. These are the spaces of spiritual realms, sometimes hidden, either in nature or ...who knows where? There is here something light, fleeting and unspoken, yet at the same time something very familiar. You can find in this piece everything which has been mentioned so far in this analysis, but perhaps not expressed directly and convincingly enough. It is like a meditation, undoubtedly filled with a longing for God, but also clearly aware of a touch of the beauty and lightness of God's grace. What matters is to discover the Unspoken in oneself again, to awaken, preserve it and to pass it on. (**Impromptu in G-flat major* op. 51)

And another thing – the question of order – specifically, its necessity and its form.

Everyone of us, arriving in this world, finds a reality which has already been given a shape. We enter a world of categories, patterns and circumstances which existed before us, and were worked out earlier by many generations and many contexts. Perforce, we must adopt an attitude to them. We reject some and accept others, identifying ourselves with them, concentrating on them, adopting them, but also leaving our own mark on them. From among the four kinds of monks St Benedict chooses just one, the cenobites, and concentrates on them. Chopin, similarly, chooses a particular set from among all the existing forms created before him, one that suits him, through which he wants to find expression. He develops it and leaves his mark on it; he makes it unique, yet recognisable and grounded in the history and tradition of his day. Significantly, it is a definite choice, reduced in essence to one instrument, but with a whole range of forms which can be realised through it. St Benedict does the same when describing different kinds of monks. He also takes up a stance in relation to the existing situation, criticising and rejecting some of the attitudes, those of the gyrovagues and sarabaites. He expresses his appreciation of the anchorites, but concentrates on the cenobites, "that most valiant kind of monks" (RulBen 1, 13).

Thus we can see that the choice itself is not everything. All it achieves (but that can be a great deal) is to define the space to be made productive, to be filled with one's own, original content. This is what happens in the case of Chopin who, concentrating on the piano, develops and perfects that instrument's idiom and expression in his own way, taking them to heights never reached before. This is what happens in the case of St Benedict. His whole *Rule* is a presentation of the widest horizons of understanding of the cenobitic form of monastic life, developing and perfecting its meaning and character, so that it is ready to reach heights never reached before.

Being able to take a detached view, to be objective about the reality in which one lives, to introduce one's own order into it and to choose the one aspect which one can "make productive," is an essential condition of consciously experiencing one's existence. This is not easy, since it requires a clear vision of the context in which we live, a good understanding of it – and courage. And yet such an attitude is necessary if we are to make the best, optimal use of our life, limited though it is in time and space.

This moment of evaluation, diagnosis and selection is what making a decision is all about. This process is taking place at practically every moment of our life, on a different scale – assuming, of course, that we try to live consciously. Each successive choice, each decision requires one to take the next step and its consequences, the new beginning it brings – together with the full range of effort and risk, of going beyond one's limits. At the same time, the choice and the beginning, the decision and its consequences, constantly intertwine and are mutually conditional. In that continuous feedback which takes place between them we may find a profile of the fundamental attitude characteristic of both monastic life and a composer's (not only Chopin's) creative attitude: openness, sensitivity, readiness, and alertness.

It is valuable and instructive to trace the process by which great artists make their personal mark on the categories which they find in existence. There can never be enough in-depth analysis of St Benedict's breadth of vision of the ideal of monastic life which existed before him. The wide spaces of the differences etched out here will always be an inexhaustible source of inspiration and delight. We can say the same about Chopin's effect on the idiom and expression of the piano, but also on the existing forms he used. The distance, at times enormous, between what he found and what he left behind in these areas is a measure of his genius – and of God's grace.

The Risk of Beginning

Undoubtedly, any activity demands the effort of making a beginning. Also, every beginning has to be begun. There is an unquestionable link between listening to music and listening to the "master's precepts". In both cases one needs sensitivity, but also an ability to concentrate and to reflect, a readiness to make constant effort of memory and imagination, to enter a world which requires commitment and sacrifice. We simply must allow that which we are listening to to pentetrate us, change us, seize us. To listen is to follow someone – to follow an idea, to leave some place behind, to start on a journey – like Abraham, like the Chosen People, like the Apostles. In such cases, the very fact of beginning the journey is an event. It requires determination and immediacy. We feel a strong, irresistible imperative. But we also feel we are seized and that, in truth, SOMEONE is leading us. We are invited, and there is no way in which we could refuse. The beginning of the first movement of *Piano concerto No. 1 in E minor* op. 11 is like that – decisive and spellbinding. From the first notes of that music we recognise the clearly delineated features of the main themes, as if two heroes of a drama taking shape before us. Everything here starts immediately, without unnecessary ceremony, yet maintaining impressive dignity and majesty:

In order to follow such a path, to allow oneself to be drawn, to be "seduced", there has to be a susceptibility, a readiness on the part of the listener, combined with experience, sensitivity and ability to concentrate. What is needed is an effective will, high degree and quality of motivation, an unquestioning availability. However, that is just one side of the coin. It is also essential that the artist should take some pains – to establish contact, to draw attention, to skilfully refer to the listener's experience or preferences, so that the latter should want to take part in the adventure of listening. If the meeting in the space of music performed and listened to is to take place, the composer and, following in his footsteps, also the performer – must undertake quite considerable effort. It is not enough to "come up with something". That "something" has to be presented, developed, given the right form to be communicated – in a word, the listener has to be taken deep into the music event itself. This is similar to the approach taken by St Benedict, who, at the beginning of his *Rule*, turns to the adept of monastic life with the following words:

> *Listen, O my son, to the precepts of thy master, and incline the ear of thy heart (...), In the first place, beg of Him by most earnest prayer, that He perfect whatever good thou dost begin (...) Let us then rise at length, since the Scripture arouseth us, saying: "It is now the hour for us to rise from sleep" (Rom 13:11); and having opened our eyes to the deifying light, let us hear with awestruck ears what the divine voice, crying out daily, doth admonish us, saying: "Today, if you shall hear his voice, harden not your hearts" (Ps 94[95]:8). And again: "He that hath ears to hear let him hear what the Spirit saith to the churches" (Rev 2:7).* (RulBen Prologue 1–15)

This is just a simple plea to listen; one, however, which reveals the whole process of listening. It is not enough to hear, what is heard must also be accepted and applied in practice. This is a complex and delicate process; difficult to capture and describe, but quite necessary. It is the first reason for the effort of listening, concentrating, accepting and applying what has been heard in one's life. It is not just the sense of hearing that is involved here, but the intellect, memory, imagination and will. We find them similarly involved and functioning integrally in music, which makes the latter a wonderful ally of Benedictine life.

However, for this to happen, it is necessary to establish contact, or even a bond, between the composer/performer and the listener. That is why the beginning is so important – and so risky.

Very often special preparation is needed to establish that contact. The right atmosphere has to be created, not just of interest, or curiosity, but, perhaps, above all, of trust. In such conditions, it is possible to be open to the correct perception and acceptance of the main motif – the factor which determines the identity and the development of a composition. Expectation takes on here a very concrete, tense character. We know that "something" will appear, but not exactly how and when. Everything is discreet and subtle, but there is a sense of inevitability about it. And everything has to take time – and the greater the danger that contact will not be established, the longer it needs to take. That is why space is needed; a space where expectations, projections, conjectures and possibilities can interact, initiating a unique game which is a germ of reality.

An illustration and a sample of its meaning can be found in a number of beginnings of Chopin's works; we can quote, for example, *Polonaise in A-flat major* op. 53:

Initially, something is being suggested, then it develops, at first shyly, then with increasing panache, leaving no doubt that what is involved is a thing that is of great import and worthy of commitment. Yes, at the beginning there is the risk of "not hitting the target", not engaging with the expectations, with the listener. The more one wants to surprise, the greater the risk. You need to be sure of your effect, yet at the same time restrain its intensity. This risks becoming "banal", but, if successful, leaves a strong impression, guaranteeing close contact between the listener and the work. The risk includes the fear of encountering a new, unfamiliar reality and the consequences this brings. The whole "taste" of risk is this constant game of tension between what is awaited, expected, and that which happens in reality. Risk, and apprehension, are also part of the decision to take up monastic life. St Benedict expresses this unequivocally in his Prologue:

> *Our hearts and our bodies must, therefore, be ready to do battle under the biddings of holy obedience; and let us ask the Lord that He supply by the help of His grace what is impossible to us by nature.* (RulBen, Prologue, 39–40)

He knew how we flinch from what appears impossible, even though it is necessary in some sense. How often we fear to continue with this or that project, to have such and such a meeting, or conversation! We are frightened of the unforeseeable, and the fear is often intensified by our prejudices. We have failed so many times; we do not believe that we will succeed now. We want to run away. Fear forces us to do so. That is why St Benedict adds:

> *We are, therefore, about to found a school of the Lord's service, in which we hope to introduce nothing harsh or burdensome. But even if, to correct vices or to preserve charity, sound reason dictateth anything that turneth out somewhat stringent, do not at once fly in dismay from the way of salvation, the beginning of which cannot but be narrow.* (Matt. 7:14). (ibid 43–45).

Every beginning demands not only great courage, but also great trust. As we can see, it usually is a relationship – it requires a response, a cooperation. We do not stand alone in the face of the unknown. The risk is shared on both sides. It seems to be an invitation to work together, to a kind of solidarity. Perhaps it is easier to face the unknown, the potential risk, when there is someone next to us who will help us cross the threshold of the unknown with delicacy and sensitivity. Everyone of us has his own threshold of sensitivity – also to effort and to pain. That is what makes mutual support possible, supplementing each other's courage and taking on the risk. There are many examples in Chopin's works of such beginnings, full of delicacy, mutual love and tenderness, an ordinary goodness which helps to bear just about anything. This is the nature of the beginning of Larghetto, i.e., the second movement of *Piano concerto in F minor* op. 21.

Another example of such delicate preparation is the beginning of *Ballade No. 4 in F minor* op. 52, where a very subtle, although suggestive motif gently leads the listener into the space of the first theme – paradoxically, even more subtle, although more clearly delineated. We are already enchanted by this initial motif. The appearance of the first theme – in a sense withdrawn and paused in its mobility – only intensifies the scale of impressions, because of the pressure on its more decisive, but simple features. The mobility which gathers later is almost "atomised", and is the means of an increasingly attractive sublimation of expectancy. The "new" which keeps appearing does not cause one to feel lost; led by the subtle lines of airy motifs, we feel safe enough to allow ourselves to be enchanted, moment after moment, without objection. Such assured delicacy seems, from another point of view, the best guide on the road to conversion.

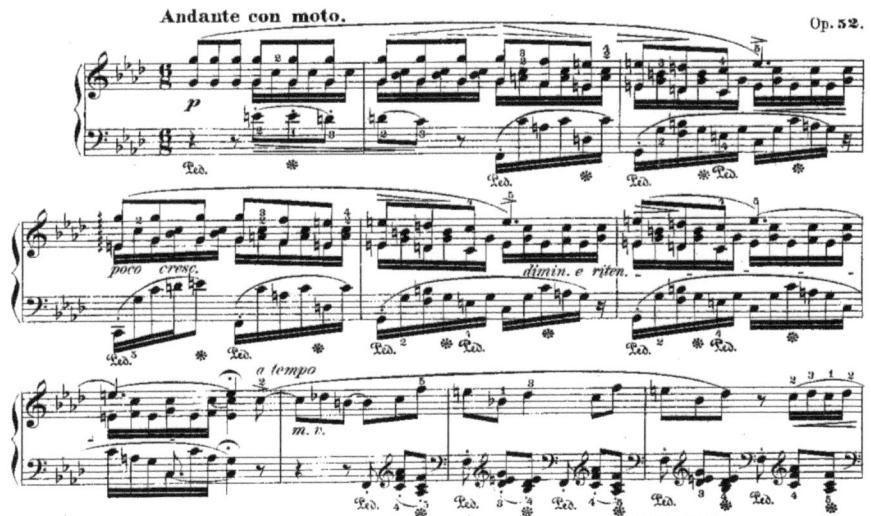

There was a song which claimed that "to love is to be lifted up". One might add that to love is to know how to start anew. Would not that be the meaning of conversion? Contained in it is the essence of the dynamism essential for normal human functioning, and also for Christianity. Such dynamism is needed to avoid stagnation. Yes, every beginning demands an effort, as does every commitment. But it is also an opportunity to participate, with full openness, in God's ceaseless creative activity. Constant beginning renews the meaning of our life. It is written into the Benedictine vow of conversion, which means nurturing a permanent inner dynamism. It is an attitude that is always relevant, and it makes mutual support in it all the more necessary. This is the only way that life can flow forward – always full of new ideas being put into practice, consistency refreshed over and over again. This is not just a matter of the beginning, but of good continuation of what it brings. It would not be an exaggeration to say that, to lead a monastic life, means to be always starting anew. And here we have an example of a very special beginning which, in its way, has a constant character, full of enthusiasm, joy and smiles. This is *Mazurka in C major* op. 7 No. 5. It is a game of beginnings which are always being reborn. Is this not a beautiful analogy of our life? To be always active and creative we must always have the courage to keep entering new, unknown areas; always keep undertaking anew collaboration with people, with God – always be ready to listen, like Abraham, like the prophets and the apostles, always on the way to unfamiliar spaces, with our great trust in God as our only support. In practice, this means constantly starting anew, and that is possible only in the space of faith which truly lets us live on hope, making love a clearly accessible reality. (**Mazurka in C major* op. 7 No. 5)

Beginnings and Trust

Every beginning is different – they beckon with their attractions; they want to surprise and to win exclusive rights. Everything depends on establishing contact and, more precisely, winning the trust of the listener. There are many ways of achieving this. Both the composer and the performer create their own paths to this goal, and the best ones are original and unique. Yet some general principles cannot be avoided. There always has to be a compromise between what is possible and what is desired. It is the final effect that counts, and in practice that is sometimes difficult to predict. That is what makes trust all the more important.

It is worthwhile paying attention to beginnings, by comparing and analysing them. Although everyone is different, we can try to group them into classes. Let us compare the beginnings of the first two waltzes from Chopin's op. 64. The first of them, in *D-flat major* (also known as the Minute Waltz), does not begin at once; it seems to be born gradually from the initial long trill A-flat –B. The motion which intensifies and becomes more dense after a few bars of hesitation, or perhaps of looking for the appropriate form, finally finds the tracks which suit it, beginning the waltz proper.

On the other hand, the next waltz, in *C-sharp minor*, begins at once. Even the first note – perhaps placed carefully and somewhat timidly – is still the beginning of a clear motif which is the first theme of the composition.

35

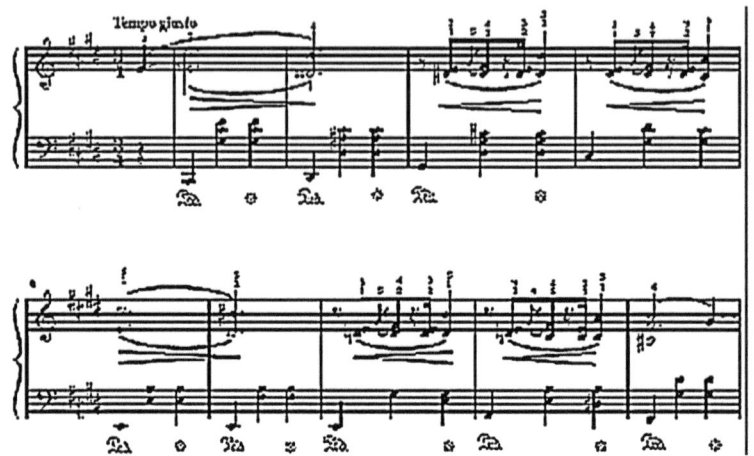

These two beginnings represent two basic ways of beginning a musical composition. They might generally be described as "with preparation" and "without". In both cases the aim is to reach the audience in the most effective manner, and to make it interested in the work. Both here and there the importance of the first contact and initial impression are fully appreciated. They determine whether the listener might be encouraged, or put off further listening. After all, everything that is new and difficult needs to be served in a special way, often preceded by appropriate preparation. In those first moments one wins the trust – or loses it. Let us listen, for instance, to the beginning of *Mazurka in C-sharp minor* op. 41 No. 1. Here also we are dealing with an introduction whose character is preparatory. It is as if Chopin is looking for the right form for the appearance of the main musical thought – as if he was formulating it live, without obligation, without guaranteeing a successful outcome, without a predetermined plan and result.

A preparatory introduction is also present in the beginning of *Scherzo in C-sharp minor* op. 39 – with the difference, however, that the composer clearly knows where he is taking the listener: the right shape of the theme seems to be dreaming, hidden somewhere, confident that soon it will be presented in all its power and beauty.

Every beginning, as we have said, is linked to risk. Its first steps – first notes – show the way in which we try to confront that risk: either with as much security as possible, with a reconnaissance of the situation and the locality; or at once, staking everything on one card. Much may depend on the character and personality of the one who begins. Certainly in both cases it is necessary to have a vision of the future – i.e., that which we want to achieve later on. Various beginnings would thus be linked to diverse strategies of presenting and realising that vision. In fact, regardless of whether the vision appears sooner or later, it must be sufficiently convincing and clear to enable the composer to underwrite it in full awareness, and that it should capture the listener. Trust, once gained, must not be lost; the promise must be kept. To gain trust is to present a vision, and to make others believe in it.

It is not enough to understand what is going on. It is necessary to take into account the expectations of the potential audience. They have to be imagined, foreseen – the more so, the more difficult the proposal we are about to present. What is important here is sensitivity, but also personal contact, consideration for the capabilities and limitations of the people to whom we speak, their prejudices. And thus, St Benedict teaches that:

> *For in his teaching the Abbot should always observe that principle of the Apostle in which he saith: "Reprove, entreat, rebuke" (2 Tm 4:2), that is, mingling gentleness with severity, as the occasion may call for, let him show the severity of the master and the loving affection of a father.* (RulBen 2, 26–29)

At another point, when talking about applying appropriate measure to everyone, he says:

> *We do not say by this that respect should be had for persons (God forbid), but regard for infirmities.* (ibid 34,1).

Every new and unknown enterprise demands particular care and a guarantee of safety, In that sense, the addressee needs security, confident leadership, and at times truly fatherly care. St Benedict makes this very clear:

> *Let him be discerning and temperate in the tasks which he enjoineth, recalling the discretion of holy Jacob who saith: "If I should cause my flocks to be overdriven, they would all die in one day" (Gen 33:13).* (RegBen 64, 18–21).

Let us think of the various beginnings in our life: about the beginning of our adulthood, our love, our vocation – and also about the beginnings of our relationships with others, our various commitments or activities. In each case some new quality was involved, and the risk linked to it, and the courage – as well as the experience, or just a touch of hope. What did we feel then? Did we think of the end result? Did we fully realise the difficulties which might threaten, or what might help? A beginning includes also the obligation to seek the path to our goal that is appropriate to our situation, with all the complexity of its contexts and conditions. Perhaps many of our failures and mistakes result from the lack of such preparation, or not exploring the path which awaited us. And, even more, from not taking into account human weakness and not humbling ourselves before it.

Paradoxically, such sensitivity to human needs and weaknesses is one of the main driving components of music. That which meets the essential needs and expectations of the human heart – that is what attracts, what enraptures. But this is what we look for when we listen to music. That is why a composer should always be humbly sensitive, and at the same time always anxious to help, to guarantee – as far as possible of course – a sense of being led, being secure. There is in it something of the attitude of a father, so very important in serving as a Benedictine abbot. At another point in the *Rule* we encounter the following, deeply moving instruction:

> *...rising to the Work of God, let them gently encourage one another on account of the excuses of the drowsy.* (RulBen 22,7).

As we can see, St Benedict recommends to the monks more than mutual obedience. He also talks about gentle mutual encouragement, and these words are spoken in the context of getting to God's service in the morning – i.e., also at the beginning of the day. This is yet another dimension of the beginning: before it is directed towards God, it should be prepared for by care for fellow brethren, full of tender gentleness, expressing the warmth of true and deep brotherly love. An example of such an attitude – or, more precisely, such care for another, for the listener, is the beginning of *Barcarolle in F-sharp major* op. 60. In fact, we have two beginnings here. The first one is the introduction into the atmosphere of the work as a whole, preparing the place for the appearance of the appropriate motifs and themes. After this gradually comes to a close, there appears what seems like the direct preparation – a presentation, by the left hand, of the melody of the accompaniment, carried out very discreetly, an invitation to the listener to give it attention and to receive favourably the main melody, which is about to appear. On the other hand, it is in this way that the said main melody, very delicate and pliant, or even trembling and weak in itself, has an opportunity of not only making a confident and effective entrance, but also of having assured support.

However, in order for the main melody, which is about to appear, to have the appropriate expressiveness and power of conviction; it must be the result of conviction and determination, a consequence of an unambiguous vision, based on clearly defined conditions of its realisation and development. One hardly needs to add that this vision should be based not only on strong motifs, but that it should be able to defend itself through its own efforts. This, in a sense, is the driving force of a composition. The work owes to it its expressiveness and originality, as well as its capacity for drawing and holding the audience's attention, involving it in the music's events. In a clearly delineated musical idea one can immediately find a spark of life. For a good and effective beginning it is thus necessary to present the basic thought, the main motif of the work, in an appropriate and intriguing manner. This, in any case, is the essence of establishing any relationship effectively, not just in a monastery. Mutual motivation should not only link the abbot with each monk, but also the monks among themselves. Thus every meeting, every taking on of a shared task, requires a good and clear beginning, so that everyone should know "what it's all about". Yes, it is primarily a matter of drawing attention, of awakening interest, but then the commitment must be maintained, and the responsibility, as well as the consequences, must be shared. Every vision is tested in this manner; it is as worthwhile as its ability to fire enthusiasm and draw people to itself. Perhaps there is no better test of a given idea than the effort of motivating and convincing that it is worth following. It is an ongoing task, a continuous process, very intense and precise. Many relationships play a part here. By motivating, we ourselves are motivated. When we have an idea, when we try to pass it on and justify it, we are forced to present it, to share it. This is a little as if we ourselves were losing it, in order to perhaps regain it, or see how quickly it falls apart. Here we can see how important is a continuous, but also honest and open exchange of thoughts and opinions. In fact, it is only in such a mutual relationship that the true and final shape of a given vision is achieved. And though it is necessary to have a person who initiates it, it is equally necessary to have those who accept the vision, and at the same time perfect it through verification.

In a Benedictine monastery, it is the abbot who should be such an initiator. It is he who shapes the vision and offers it to his fellow brethren. The "feedback" is provided by the institution of council, provided for by St Benedict in the third chapter of the *Rule*. If contact can be established along that line, there is a high likelihood that the "play" of monastic life will move from the phase of being an idea to being accepted and applied in practice.

Here are some examples of beginnings, where an idea presented unambiguously awakens our immediate trust and enables a convincing shaping of the work. This is because here we experience something very clear and obvious and, because of this, sufficiently intriguing that we just have to "enter" into the whole affair. There are no questions. Only a deep touch of grace and encounter with it in its space. This is what happens in *Mazurka in B-flat major* op. 7 No.1, where that original vision has a determined character.

It can also be more delicate, and because of that perhaps even more charming, as in *Mazurka in E minor* op. 41 No 2.

And, finally, it can be so clear and powerful that it carries one off from the first moment of its appearance. Is that not what happens in *Polonaise in A major* op. 40 No. 1?

One can learn a lot from Chopin in terms of sensitivity and ability to detect the nuances of the listeners' expectations and preferences. Similarly, St Benedict is a master of making beginnings – particularly when difficult and complex matters are involved. This can be seen in the beginnings of the chapters of his *Rule*, including the first one. St Benedict is very clear here: *there are four kinds of monks* (RulBen 1,1). He simply starts with the matter in hand, without unnecessary introductions – those were made in the Prologue, what is left now is concreteness itself. The same applies to the beginning of the second chapter, *What kind of man the Abbot ought to be*:

> *The Abbot who is worthy to be over a monastery, ought always to be mindful of what he is called, and make his works square with his name of Superior. For he is believed to hold the place of Christ in the monastery, when he is called by his name, according to the saying of the Apostle: "You have received the spirit of adoption of sons, whereby we cry Abba (Father)" (Rom 8:15).* (RulBen 2, 1–4).

Only the greatest can begin in this way. They simply tell what they see – they present the reality revealed to them, in which, and with regard to which, there is no doubt and no hesitation. The third chapter of the *Rule* has a similar beginning:

> *Whenever weighty matters are to be transacted in the monastery, let the Abbot call together the whole community, and make known the matter which is to be considered. Having heard the brethren's views, let him weigh the matter with himself and do what he thinketh best.* (RulBen, 3, 1–2)

And again – the beginning comes immediately, without unnecessary preparations. That is always a very valuable gift, which we should constantly wish for, particularly those of us who are in any way in charge of others. At the same time, we must always realise that all our beginnings are human. It is only God for whom the problem of the beginning does not exist. He himself does not have a beginning, being an eternal beginning and at the same time the eternal end, Alpha and Omega, as the New Testament tells us. It is we who find our beginning in Him, while we are destined to make beginnings, and to struggle with them. We have to accept it in humility and openness to God's grace. We should always be learning to withdraw ourselves into God and to lose ourselves in the adoration of Him. It is only thus that we shall be given the eternal freshness of a constant and always enticing beginning, the touch of the inexpressible breath of the Holy Spirit. Through this we shall know how to begin without making a beginning, simply to reveal. There are a number of Chopin's works which reflect this situation in an incomparable way. For example, *Etude in G-sharp minor* op. 25 No. 6, which has in it a spellbinding breath of eternity, almost magical in its simplicity yet at the same time is quite extraordinary. If you listen carefully, you can hear in it a penetrating gust of wind, the rustle of the procession of snowflakes, those little circlets, so fleeting and mysterious. There is no beginning here, just the pure breath: *You hear its sound, but you cannot tell where it comes from or where it is going* (John 3,8). There is something so obvious about it that there is nothing to think about – as if an unexpected touch of the inner pulse of the Spirit, which can be scared away in a moment. (**Etude in G-sharp minor* op. 25 No. 6)

Authority

A beginning – although, as we tried to show, it involves effort – leads to other efforts, and even harder ones. Before we take them on, a basic condition must be met: we must be aware of the direction and the goal of the proposed activities. This is a matter of having authority, and that is what we need to consider now. In a Benedictine community, this is naturally linked to the office of abbot. At the same time, however, this is a quality which is necessary for any shared activity, not to mention a shared life. The presence of authority is thus necessary both for the undertaking and for effective implementation of any project, as well as for loving others effectively, for expressing and giving that love in a way that is convincing and effective, clearly and harmoniously.

Paraphrasing the words of St Irenaeus of Lyon, we might say that God plays the harp of the human story with two hands, Jesus Christ and the Holy Spirit. To stay within the sphere of Chopin's music, we might say that it is more like playing the piano. In either case, the image of God making music was very dear to the Church Fathers. Undoubtedly also because it beautifully combines – as does music – the various aspects of human activity, including the matter of authority. A musician-instrumentalist (but not only) is a powerful icon of authority. In a sense, one can learn a lot from music, even with regard to exerting authority. One might say that a person with authority should resemble a musician more than a painter.

In one Benedictine monastery the monks chose a painter as their abbot. He was a very talented artist who, having decided to enter a monastery, destroyed nearly all his works and decided not to paint again. This does not mean, however, that he succeeded in shedding his painterly sensitivity and a painter's way of seeing, as well as organising, the world; for a talented artist this would seem to be an integral part of his nature. When he was no longer abbot – knowing that a tumour would soon put an end to his life – he said to the newly elected abbot, this time a musician by education: "I think that, as a musician, you will find it easier than I did. I was always tormented by the visual need to order space, which I always tried to control. I was being destroyed by chaos, as well as by everything which eluded my control. On the other hand, a musician should be better able to cope with the unpredictable human element, as he is accustomed to constantly controlling the corrections to the reality which is being shaped."

Undoubtedly this is a very perceptive comment, which might serve as another justification for the claim of kinship between spirituality and music. In fact, a visual imagination does constantly strive to organise space precisely and to perfection. Most often this is done at the level of an individual, i.e., through the efforts of a particular artist, whose responsibility it is not only to arrive at arbitrary solutions, but who is almost obsessively unable to bear vagueness, and the temporary nature of any form of chaos. On the other hand, a musician, from the beginning to the end, must maintain contact with the material to which he is giving shape. The result of his work is always dependent on other people – not just the soloist, but also the composer, as well as members of the orchestra and chamber ensembles. Returning to the question of authority, this involves not just responsibility, but also – and perhaps primarily – the ability to constructively shape human relationships. Moreover, a musician seems to be prepared for this by the nature of his profession. Dealing with music, he is perfectly aware of the importance of the beginning and the necessity of establishing and maintaining contact with the listener. A painter usually works alone, and does not have to be able to share the responsibility with others for the work which is being created.

The above remarks may serve as an introduction to the actual discourse on the subject of authority, and how it is to be understood in the office of abbot, or any other person in a position of power. We have mentioned the necessity of having a clear and convincing vision. This must be followed by the ability to realise it in specific circumstances, i.e., the ability to cooperate with others towards a goal, to motivate and direct them, with the full awareness of the risk involved, the possibility of error or even of failure. All this must be encompassed within the feeling of responsibility. Every time we have an idea, when we come to put it into practice we automatically submit it to judgment, to the crticism of others, as well as to the possibility of rejection. This is inevitable, regardless of who puts forward a given idea or project. Perhaps it is even the case that the greater the authority, the greater the risk and the pressure of external opinion. We can thus see that, in order to achieve a planned goal, one has to keep working on maintaining the trust, the patience, as well as determination and motivation. But that is not possible with just the support of human resources, but, rather, only with the help of divine grace and intervention. It is thus hardly surprising that the guarantee of authority is provided by its support in an authority higher than the natural one. Within the context of the Benedictine order, this means that the abbot should, above all, be a man of prayer. What this really means is that he should always be able to draw, without obstacle, on that higher source when fulfilling his duty.

A vivid illustration of an attitude of sufficiently strong grounding in Transcendence to enable appropriate and effective breadth of vision in presenting and realising an idea is the *Finale* of Chopin's *Piano sonata No. 3 in B minor* op. 58.

This is an image of tremendous and impressive motion, gathering and moving through various forms, and a pulsation of phrases which constantly rise and fall. It is an organised motion, but it also makes use of elemental spontaneity. Confidence is combined here with openness and daring, consistency and patience with power and determination. In this music, which is an irresistible flow of variations and constantly accumulating climaxes, one can discern an outline, or a reflection of the triumphal progress of Jehovah – a panoramic Epiphany strikingly shown in Psalm 68(67). In this image we can also find echoes of another march – that of the Israelites across the desert, as well as various epopees of the prophets, and then, in the New Testament, the paths of the Apostles and the Church. These paths are not easy, but only in this way can God's power and glory be revealed to the full. At the same time, this is the paths of trust and hope being constantly born anew, creating an ever closer bond between man and God:

Let God arise, let his enemies be scattered: let them also that hate him flee before him. As smoke is driven away, so drive them away: as wax melteth before the fire, so let the wicked perish at the presence of God.

But let the righteous be glad; let them rejoice before God: yea, let them exceedingly rejoice. Sing unto God, sing praises to his name: extol him that rideth upon the heavens by his name JAH, and rejoice before him.

A father of the fatherless, and a judge of the widows, is God in his holy habitation.

God setteth the solitary in families: he bringeth out those which are bound with chains: but the rebellious dwell in a dry land.

O God, when thou wentest forth before thy people, when thou didst march through the wilderness; Selah:

The earth shook, the heavens also dropped at the presence of God: even Sinai itself was moved at the presence of God, the God of Israel.

Thou, O God, didst send a plentiful rain, whereby thou didst confirm thine inheritance, when it was weary.

Thy congregation hath dwelt therein: thou, O God, hast prepared of thy goodness for the poor.

The Lord gave the word: great was the company of those that published it.

Kings of armies did flee apace: and she that tarried at home divided the spoil.

Though ye have lien among the pots, yet shall ye be as the wings of a dove covered with silver, and her feathers with yellow gold.

When the Almighty scattered kings in it, it was white as snow in Salmon.

The hill of God is as the hill of Bashan; an high hill as the hill of Bashan.

Why leap ye, ye high hills? this is the hill which God desireth to dwell in; yea, the LORD will dwell in it for ever.

The chariots of God are twenty thousand, even thousands of angels: the Lord is among them, as in Sinai, in the holy place.

Thou hast ascended on high, thou hast led captivity captive: thou hast received gifts for men; yea, for the rebellious also, that the LORD God might dwell among them.

Blessed be the Lord, who daily loadeth us with benefits, even the God of our salvation. Selah.

He that is our God is the God of salvation; and unto God the Lord belong the issues from death.

But God shall wound the head of his enemies, and the hairy scalp of such an one as goeth on still in his trespasses.

The Lord said, I will bring again from Bashan, I will bring my people again from the depths of the sea:

That thy foot may be dipped in the blood of thine enemies, and the tongue of thy dogs in the same.

They have seen thy goings, O God; even the goings of my God, my King, in the sanctuary.

The singers went before, the players on instruments followed after; among them were the damsels playing with timbrels.

Bless ye God in the congregations, even the Lord, from the fountain of Israel.

There is little Benjamin with their ruler, the princes of Judah and their council, the princes of Zebulun, and the princes of Naphtali.

Thy God hath commanded thy strength: strengthen, O God, that which thou hast wrought for us.

Because of thy temple at Jerusalem shall kings bring presents unto thee.

Rebuke the company of spearmen, the multitude of the bulls, with the calves of the people, till every one submit himself with pieces of silver: scatter thou the people that delight in war.

Princes shall come out of Egypt; Ethiopia shall soon stretch out her hands unto God.

Sing unto God, ye kingdoms of the earth; O sing praises unto the Lord; Selah:

To him that rideth upon the heavens of heavens, which were of old; lo, he doth send out his voice, and that a mighty voice.

Ascribe ye strength unto God: his excellency is over Israel, and his strength is in the clouds.

O God, thou art terrible out of thy holy places: the God of Israel is he that giveth strength and power unto his people. Blessed be God.

In this psalm – as in the finale of *Sonata in B minor* – there is much enthusiasm. However, that enthusiasm is very demanding; it is born, and it develops, because of the difficulties. Continually increasing, it not only keeps us moving forward, but also keeps providing inspiration and enrichment. This constant dynamism is necessary in any managerial position. It demonstrates very accurately that which is the concern of the second chapter of the *Rule*, when the instructions and the teaching of the abbot are compared to the *leaven of divine justice* which is meant to leave a permanent mark in the hearts of the disciples. Although the comparison itself has a static character, it hides within a very deep and fundamental dynamism. This is why it is so important to be aware of the existence and the action of that dynamism – all the more so when we apply it to a person directing a community, i.e., the one who implements God's will within it in practical terms. Let us therefore quote again the beginning of the second chapter of the *Rule* referred to earlier for different reasons:

> *The Abbot who is worthy to be over a monastery, ought always to be mindful of what he is called, and make his works square with his name of Superior. For he is believed to hold the place of Christ in the monastery, when he is called by his name...* (RulBen 2, 1–3).

(**Piano sonata in B minor* op. 58, Finale. Presto non tanto)

To be the leaven, the "shaping principle", means taking the position of a particular kind of intermediary. On the one hand, one really must have within oneself the content, the core, the root of inspiration which gives the base, the "leaven", its identity. On the other – one has to help that which is the most essential to spread within the "leavening" space as far and as well as possible. One thus has to be able to demonstrate and transmit something important, of which one is an honest depositary and carrier. In a musical composition, this is the role of the main theme, which carries the fundamental musical content of the work as a whole, or its larger part. In a Benedictine monastery, such "leaven", such a "shaping principle" is the abbot. He is the one who interprets the *Rule*, who determines the shape of the monks' everyday lives.

Hence another invitation to listen – and to meditate. Here is another composition which has the character of a portrait of a person with authority – an abbot who tries to put into practice a synthesis of the values which are most important for life as a Benedictine: dignity, grace, strength, as well as sweetness and kindness. We start in a very delicate way – since it is necessary to establish contact – including those for whom the superior is responsible. This is the nature of the beginning of *Mazurka in C-sharp minor* op. 63 No. 3. The simple but clearly delineated melody, although not forceful, has in it some power which draws attention and orders one to follow it. That same gentle and clear motif is repeated time and again – or, rather, it unhesitatingly leads the flow of the melody. There is about it something flexible and sensitive, a grace and a consistency, patience mixed with some resignation or even nostalgia, a sadness about being helpless and ineffective, a humility and discretion.

Authority – particularly that of an abbot – should be characterised by a delicate and sensitive approach. However, it should not be devoid of strength. The strength which manifests itself in delicacy and sensitivity that we have in mind here is particularly well conveyed in *Andante Spianato* and *Grand polonaise in E-flat major* op. 22. It is, in a sense, a treatise on the exercise of power, on being the boss, on authority. Metaphorically, it presents the full range of means and strategies which are necessary – and desirable – when holding power. Everything begins in a friendly atmosphere of great calm and balance. The narration, conducted subtly and gracefully yet consistently, demonstrates not only control over the situation, but also over the emotions. Here, tenderness and gentleness carry a special freshness. They are imbued with an inner dynamism, which is controlled and restrained at all times. At one point, however, there is an explosion of decisiveness and power, when the clearly delineated introduction opens the Grand Polonaise. Here, the situation changes totally. It is dominated by determination, at times close to anger. All of this takes place in an unchanging aura of abundant ideas. Nobility is combined here with lightness, power with grace. This should be the character of a person with authority, so aptly described by St Benedict in chapters 2 and 64 of his *Rule*, which are devoted to the duties of the abbot. One might say that the Grand Polonaise orchestrates the demanding composition of the guidelines provided by the author of the *Rule*. It becomes a metaphor for a synthesis of values which need to characterise a person holding authority: dignity, the power of sweetness, as well as the constant listening and adapting to the requirements and the needs of the weakest. Sensitivity and delicacy are, perhaps the fullest expression of the power of authority.

(*Andante Spianato and Grand Polonaise in E-flat major* op. 22 (*))

Weakness

A necessary complement to having authority seems to be that which is at the opposite pole, i.e., surrender, defencelessness, weakness. Always present, weakness is important in providing a counterweight to the power which goes with authority. It is a constant test and verification of authority, which, in its way, is confirmed by the words from chapter 64 of St Benedict's *Rule* (quoted earlier), about the need for an abbot to maintain empathy and moderation: "bearing in mind the discretion of holy Jacob, who said, *If I cause my flocks to be overdriven, they will all die in one day.*" (RegBen 64, 19–21).

Everyone, not just those belonging to the Benedictine community, has his measure. Weakness is, on the one hand, a lack of strength, and on the other, lack of perseverance, and thus consistency. Weakness is necessary so that space can be created for pity or for mercy. Only the strong can show pity and be merciful, by being sensitive to the weaknesses and shortcomings which they have the opportunity to overcome. It happens quite often that conflicted, aggressive persons are in reality simply very weak. And the reverse is true – those who are calm and moderate turn out also to be very strong. Weakness is thus necessary to reveal to us our situation and the condition we are in. We may thus talk about the importance of weakness and even, in a sense, about its ...beauty. In this context we may talk about weakness as an icon of Christ – an image of Jesus hidden in others, in those who suffer – in their helplessness, pain and suffering.

Ryszard Przybylski describes Chopin's music as "a response to human spiritual drama"[9]. The composer himself expressed it in his own, very plastic and more earthy manner: "it is not my fault that I am like that mushroom, like a champignon, which poisons when you dig it out of the earth and taste it, taking it for something else – I know that I have never been of any use to anyone – but not of much use to myself either."[10] There is much humility and bitterness in these words. But this is exactly what makes them so near to us – as if they were our own.

There are two examples of Chopin's music which depict human weakness in a very moving way. Their authenticity and simplicity are striking. Where weakness

---

9   R. Przybylski, *Cień jaskółki*, p. 217.
10   R. Przybylski, *Cień jaskółki*, s. 217.10 Quoted after R. Przybylski, ibid., p. 217. *Korespondencja Fryderyka Chopina*, vol. I, Collected and edited by B.E. Sydow, Warszawa 1955, p. 337, from a letter to Julian Fontana, written in Marseille on 7 March 1839.

appears, words have no place. And perhaps only music has the right to try and touch it – or perhaps rather, to express the weakness – of course, as far as it is possible. Firstly, *Mazurka in F minor* op. 68 No. 4. This is Chopin's last piece, written almost on his deathbed. It is full of modulations, uncertainties, hesitations, moments suspended – it seems to be an echo of a search ... without a goal, an instability, a longing for a point of support. (**Mazurka in F minor* op. 68 No. 4)

And there is also *Prelude in C-sharp minor* op. 45, where in turn we find even more numerous modulations, in a sense more obsessive ones, as if they were trying to show that the composer still has quite a lot of strength, enough to search, yearn, or even lose his way. This work seems to be woven from constant changes and uncertainties. (**Prelude in C-sharp minor* op. 45)

It is worthwhile listening from time to time to just such a composition in order to develop our sensitivity and understanding of those who are weaker, who need support not only physically but – perhaps primarily – emotionally or psychologically. This is because human weakness often results from various confused and unresolved feelings, ambitions or complexes. Whether we want to or not, a shared life, in one group or another, can only, of necessity, be built on the foundations of human frailty and weakness. This will always be a challenge which is demanding and, in its way, cruel. The structure of any organisation must, of necessity, be based on individuals who are weak and who make mistakes.

At one monastery, one of the monks, always very practical, very well organised and effective in his actions, was always very impatient. This concerned people and their behaviour, as well as external circumstances. And so he pointed to the need of reforming the monastic structures, to make them function better and more effectively. The suggestion was very apt, and thus they tried to take up this challenge. Towards this aim, the superiors of this monastery, encouraged by their superintendent, contacted a consultant on company management and organisation. Together with him, they conducted an in-depth analysis of the practical possibilities of developing the monastery and the tasks it could undertake. It turned out that a monastery is a very complex and untypical organisation. However, after long reflection and numerous attempts it turned out to be also possible to work out a model of how monastic structures function. When everything was ready on paper, the consultant felt obliged to confess honestly that the most problematic area of every structure, however well designed, are simply the people. They can never be arranged or programmed one hundred percent. They will always remain as they are, with their limitations and weaknesses, and even the best organised structures will not help that. This, of course, does not mean that we should give up trying to improve structures; it is simply that human weakness is so important and ... so strong, that we will always have to take it into consideration. His superiors thus told the fellow brother who was so keen on change, when he gave vent to his impatience and displeasure over the lack of effectiveness of the changes, that people were not little tin soldiers or puppets. Unfortunately ... or fortunately. Any management of a human team demands that one takes into account the unpredictable parameter relating to the "human factor". Most often it is unreliability or limitedness – or ordinary, unplanned weakness. These, human considerations, are the most frequent cause of difficulties in life. They constitute a constant challenge for each of us. At the same time, however, and paradoxically, they protect our life from being completely mechanical and automatic – something that we would probably not wish for. For this reason, we are to some extent "condemned" to our own weakness, which in the context described above helps to release us. If that is the case, we must continuously keep finding in ourselves new layers of trust, patience and hope – so that we can see others and the future in a positive light.

There are many weaknesses that go unnoticed, not understood, with no chance of being supported. It is often a weakness of open wounds or hidden or undeserved suffering. We should always be sensitive and alert, since there is a very fine borderline between weakness and sloth. Sometimes the inability or limitation are to a much greater degree a matter of choice or the result of passivity rather than an actual, organic or external obstacle. It is thus truly difficult to decide with certainty whether someone is not doing something because they are unable to do it, or whether they simply do not want to do it. This is a second level – or the false bottom – of weakness: it hides itself, masks itself, leaving in its place a hole in the system, disturbing the functioning of the surrounding relationships. One is forced to search, to intervene, to be active. Often desperately so, but that makes it all the more moving. That is the nature of *Mazurka in A minor* op. 7 No. 2. Even the motif which begins it, intended as a forerunner of the accompaniment, is not given its final, full shape: it remains, at best, open, if not amorphous. In a moment the main melody overlays it; that also seems to be searching for its identity; it seems to keep breaking down, pausing, lurking. It appears to try to save itself with ornamentation, which highlights its weakness – and that in some ways is very appealing!

One can also often observe and experience what might be described as "deformed" weakness. It is difficult to understand, and all the more so to treat, since it often originates from our complexes or internal blockages, unhealthy ambitions or frustrations. For this reason we usually avoid confrontation with weakness, either ours or other people's, pretending that we do not see it, or not taking it seriously when we do see it. Weakness in itself is a kind of deformation. There is no model, "classic" form of weakness – each one is uncomfortable in a unique way, becoming a kind of challenge. It is puzzling that modern art seems to delight in the subject of deformation, treated in a variety of ways. Perhaps that is because it is increasingly difficult to find out what the norm is supposed to be, and everything seems to be standing more and more on its head? Modern visual arts, music and literature result from a multitude of views of deformation: they give witness to deformation, or rather to amorphism, and to a reality that increasingly eludes our standards and our control. We may find this situation in art acceptable or not, we may pretend that the problem does not exist, even though this is a fact, a very clear (however problematic) sign of our times. Perhaps it would be too much of a simplification to describe it as the "cry of contemporaneity", or as one aspect of human condition that is highly damaged, not only existentially or emotionally. Each one of us experiences every day many forms of more or less apparent deformation or destruction. This happens in practically every human group. That is why we need to be very humble and extremely delicate, so as not to obstruct the opening of this space of deformation to the healing action of God. In perhaps only this aspect, this is a privileged space. St Benedict understood and described it very well, pointing to the powerful horizon of prayer:

> ... it is not in many words, but in the purity of heart and tears of compunction that we are heard. (RulBen 20, 3–4).

As we can see, weakness, in its lack of fulfilment, can break into openness. It then becomes an opportunity for something more. Who knows, perhaps that is its ultimate goal? Maybe that is how the space of empathy is created, perhaps even more, of goodness and love?

Maybe the enigmatic *Prelude in A minor* op. 28 No. 2 would be easier to understand in such categories. This is music which might give the impression of being "deformed", yet at the same time it sounds almost very contemporary, as well as being very moving. It is delicate in its roughness, discreet in its puzzlement. As if it wanted to touch, timidly, some difficult human existential situation. (**Prelude in A minor* op. 28 No. 2)

We are all just fragile elements of a larger whole, a structure which "has to" be based on weakness, condemning itself in this way to a constant threat of deformation.

This teaches humility on both sides. One should not expect great things either from above or below. And yet one has to exist, create, be constructive in spite of everything. Weakness is perhaps necessary to make us maintain the alertness and the sensitivity that we need. It creates an opportunity for acquiring genuine strength – not the human one, fundamentally mired in various deformations, but the one which allows one to rise above the deformations and act in spite of them. The experience of weakness is, after all, as has been said before, a privileged place of prayer, revelation and contemplation of God hidden in us and among us. Weakness is an always open invitation to pity and mercy. This is its only "strong" side, which is also potentially one of the few functioning aspects of the reality contaminated by human deformations. Encounters with weakness may teach us humility, openness, sensitivity to others, to that which is human, to God. Experiencing humiliating limitations, we may recognise the suffering God within us.

In our times, in the face of an explosive accumulation of evidence of human weakness, deformation and destruction, it is becoming progressively easier to come to the conclusion (which, by the way, is not new) that God is dead. Confused, we have neither the courage nor the strength to look for positives. All the more need for humility in order to discern them. One of them is the strong and moving testimony of a 28-year-old Jewish woman from Holland, Etty Hillesum, who was murdered in Auschwitz in 1943. She was a clever and sensitive girl, who did not practise her religion but was open to people and to love. Moved by the suffering which befell her nation, she took it up as a challenge. Ultimately this turned out to be the path to discovering the necessity of the existence of God. It was only in this way that she could regain inner harmony within the nightmare which she and her people were living through because of Auschwitz. Etty left behind her diary and letters.[11] Through the painful record of her experiences and her search for hope comes the idea – shocking yet so close to our hearts – that during the times when God seems absent, man should help Him by his attitude – as God's collaborator and witness – restoring faith in Him. It is thus necessary to endure the suffering, to bear the weakness, to carry on through the often cruel deformations, the consequences of which touch us in a tragic manner. The writings of Etty Hillesum testify that this is a mystical path of opening oneself to intimate contact with God in a space constituted by the absurd.

It is perhaps in this spirit that one should listen to Chopin's unusual *Nocturne in G minor* op. 15 No. 3. It is unusual in that the classic nocturne form ABA, which consists in closing the composition by repeating its first part, is disturbed (not

---

11   E. Hillesum, *An Interrupted Life the Diaries 1941–1943*, and *Letters from Westerbork*. New York 1996.

to say "deformed"). In such cases the second (middle) part is usually contrasted with the outlying ones; this seems obvious from the point of view of perception, and is a principle to which Chopin always adhered in an innovative and at the same time masterly manner. On this occasion, this principle is broken, primarily because the second part is quieter than the first, which in the case of a nocturne, a form of "night" music, i.e. very quiet music – is somewhat of an innovation. This nocturne displays a degree of obsessiveness in its first part. The phrases are short, determined, even violent. The second (contrasting) part, marked *religioso*, brings a calming of the melodic line by lengthening the phrases and making them more gentle. A chorale seems to be present here, and thus an undoubted reference to church music, to a space of concentration, inner ardour, prayer. If we juxtapose the sound of this chorale with the somewhat convulsive expression of the first part of the nocturne, we may interpret it as an expression of the search for healing, an inner effort to overcome one's own weakness, an attempt to transform it into a transcendent reality. It is thus hardly surprising that the first part is not repeated. Ultimately, the initial, somewhat obsessive, uncertainty is overcome by inner peace and concentration. The second part seems to pass into, "flow into" the third, replacing it altogether. One might say that in this way the idea of the nocturne, i.e., quiet night music, is saved, even though initially it did not seem likely. We can only wish that this should always be the final perspective on the weaknesses and deformations we experience.

(**Nocturne in G minor* op. 15 No. 3)

Interactions and Relationships

Everything that links us to other people can be found not only around weakness, but also on its edges. This is an extremely important and current issue. We already know, having got to know Chopin's music, how important it is to allow space to the others, preparing for their arrival and for meeting them. This is not an exceptional situation, but everyday reality, a constant component of our life – perhaps a further consequence of a good beginning that we talked about earlier. Both we ourselves, and everyone around us, need time, space, but also attention, understanding and acceptance.

Listening to music is similar. We may discover how much it teaches us in terms of sensitivity, delicacy, as well as the wisdom of life shared with others. How is that possible? We know that music is "composed", as the name indicates, of component parts, of simpler elements of specific importance – the main motif, main theme, secondary theme, bridge, accompaniment etc. It is worthwhile to observe how they make their appearance, how they link up, how they relate to each other, and how the composer treats them. Even a slight degree of sensitivity to music enables one to hear that various relationships take place between individual musical segments, and we can describe them in categories similar to those which describe our relationships with people. Let us take as an example *Barcarolle in F sharp major* op. 60, already mentioned previously. It is a picturesque and suggestive image from Venice, where we can feel the motion of the waves, the delicate but bracing stirring of the breeze, the brilliance of the sun. All this is stretched out between the two basic themes, the notes of which form the *Barcarolle.* These themes are linked by some inner kinship, but at the same time their appearance is divided by a proper distance, the appropriate space which seems to be filled with respect. Discretion guarantees closeness here, while the motion and the rhythmic fluidity which follow from it allow the boundaries to be clearly established. Let us hear how much care is devoted to the preparation and introduction of the first, and then the second theme of that *Barcarolle*. The first theme emerges from the initially denser, then more diluted, intensity of motion. The second theme gathers itself from the growing, undulating rhythm. The motion remains the same, but its shape, form and intensity undergo a change. (The example is at the beginning of the next page).

Here is another example – *Nocturne in E major* op. 62 No. 2. It begins with seeming diffidence, but its elegance becomes perceptible quite quickly. The first part of this nocturne, which keeps throughout within the rhythmic outline

sketched at the beginning, seems to rise delicately in the episode which follows, with a motion that initially seeps through timidly but with time fills ever greater space, ultimately to find release in the daring, multi-threaded middle part of the work. It is as if a place was being gradually prepared for that middle part, so that it could resound to the full. When it does appear, it can draw all our attention to itself, and when it begins its exit, it will turn again into the measured but graceful calm of the first part. Here can be heard the direct return of the main theme: having made room for the middle part, it does not need a special space for itself. The only thing it seems to still want is to prepare the phrase of the ending itself. It is therefore not surprising that we hear again the humble, mobile episode from the bridge which comes between the two parts. (*Nocturne in E major* op. 62 No. 2)

This music appears to explain the necessity of preserving appropriate spaces in our relationships. The composer always has to take into account the individual elements of a work, their varying weight and the proportions to be preserved between them. In our life also, there are elements which are more or less important, alien, at times intrusive. This demands of us constant alertness and care over the right proportions of attention, of commitment – the appropriate space. Taking into account the "otherness" of another may be a healing and inspiring experience, on condition that, prior to it, we make sufficient effort to ensure the proper place for it, clearly defining the space which both joins and divides us. Otherwise we ourselves, our life, our "little world" will be threatened.

One thus has to acknowledge clearly the presence of the blessed difficulty of being together, of the shared coexistence and collaboration. Needing another person and a relationship with them, we must at the same time accept various forms of "invasion" by another – or at least the constant stress and difficulty of creating the right conditions for meeting them. One need only observe carefully our first reactions to unexpected encounters with other people and draw one's conclusions. Even if we want to justify ourselves by claiming ignorance, this does not change the fact that the problem, or rather the challenge, remains always relevant. What do we feel when another person appears on the horizon? What do we think when someone asks us to meet them? What are the dominant feelings: fear and suspicion, or openness and joy? Perhaps we are afraid that someone has some business with us – perhaps blaming us for something (this most probably is the standard reaction when in a group of people living together, such as in a company, the boss wants to talk to someone)? Perhaps they will ask us for something – something that will take up time and bring new stresses? Probably our experience of encounters with other people are basically negative.

That is why the prospect of each new contact naturally evokes fear first of all. Naturally, the possibility of any encounter, with anybody, always brings an element of risk, an embryo of potential difficulties. But this seems unavoidable, and perhaps necessary. Condemned to living together, we must mutually accept various forms of the presence of others. This works both ways, and is not only the basis of the art of dialogue, but a condition of our practical functioning in the world. After all, we do not just live together. We also have to act together. The art of working together is perhaps even more difficult than being together with someone. Yet these days one can only act effectively as a group, the times of solo performers and lone discoverers is past. Yes, charismatic individuals are needed, but the condition of their success is always the presence of a group in the background.

Perhaps it was the need of "the other", of support or collaboration, understood one way or another that contributed to the rise of polyphony. Perhaps it is for this reason that Chopin – but also other composers of the Romantic period, that era of extreme individualism – sometimes reached for polyphony, which meant surrendering to the greater discipline necessary to functioning in a group.

This is what happened both with Mozart and with Beethoven. An increasingly vocal independence, a sense of one's own dignity and freedom, somehow do not seem self-sufficient. A single melodic line, with an accompaniment subordinated to it, has all it takes to satisfy individual aspirations almost without limit. In polyphony, however, one also has to take into account the importance of other voices or melodic lines. This happens according to strictly defined principles, which have to be followed in a consistent and disciplined manner, obeying the wider perspective. It is very interesting that the highly individualised genius of Mozart or Chopin felt, every now and then, the need to humbly undertake the demands of discipline and external principles – perhaps in order to express more, a new quality which arises from coexistence and collaboration of many various elements.

Let us take two examples. It is important to note that the polyphonic fragments introduced by Chopin are always basically at the heart of the composition – perhaps in order to express something particularly significant, something that requires special preparation. Admittedly, these are not numerous, but they are usually very meaningful fragments of Chopin's important works – perhaps decisive for the development of his work in general. This applies to the beginning of *Mazurka in C-sharp minor* op. 50 No. 3, or the stretto in *Ballade No. 4 in F minor* op. 51, as well as the middle part of *Nocturne in E major* op. 62 No.1 mentioned earlier. In the first of these works, polyphony appears exceptionally at the beginning, imparting a focused character to the start of the narration. At the same time, the dialogue integral to its nature implies openness, and heralds a new perspective.

In the case of the ballad or the nocturne, the polyphonic section appears as a culmination, a closure of the growing tension. It brings a moment of halting, of withdrawal, but – again, as in the case of the mazurka mentioned a little while ago – it imparts a new dimension to the quality of expression. In the case of the ballad we have no difficulty in recognising the main theme "shorn" of ornamentation and accompaniment, intertwining (conducting a dialogue?) with itself. This happens for a moment. Everything is suspended, the current, rising flow of expression is halted. A moment later homophony and the previous manner of expression return.

In the case of *Nocturne in E major* the polyphonic segment is more expanded. It forms an independent part, all the more important since it was prepared for by the expanded first part. The contrast is thus all the greater; it is created by a multitude of melodic lines intertwining with each other, and the intensity of motion and expression that this brings.

What purpose does this serve? Perhaps it illustrates the necessity of dialogue, the need to tame difficult and demanding contacts by submitting to specific rules with the right degree of sensitivity and humility. In order to successfully establish contact with someone, one thus needs to submit to rules, to pay more attention to one's impressions, to cultivate greater sensitivity and concentration. However, a necessary condition, and a beginning of this, is the art of listening. In both cases an intense effort is required – but one that is worthwhile, since its ultimate purpose is to serve the creation of a dialogue.

In Chopin's music we also find examples of the work carried out by the subordinate aspect of a composition, the "background", which helps to create the right atmosphere and the space for dialogue. Sometimes, in order to meet someone, or to achieve real contact with someone, some preparatory work is needed. Sometimes it takes many years to achieve the right space of trust, the right atmosphere or level of good will. Humility will always be needed in the service of meeting and dialogue, but also a certain sensitivity, delicacy and the ability to weave together the invisible threads needed to prepare that which is most important in the encounter.

Very often in our life we must perform gestures, or work towards something in which we will not share. We have to provide the backing for someone who will complete our actions – dot the "i's" and cross the "t's", or simply "cream off" the result. Often this means working not so much "for" someone else, as preparing the ground for them. Organising someone's concert, or some public event, demands a great deal of such preparatory effort – incommensurate with what is seen (and/or heard) in the event itself. Although most people prefer to be visible, to be in the first line, inevitably the numbers of those working in the background must be incommensurably greater. The majority of activities which go towards making a particular event happen concerns precisely that backing and support which remains invisible and sometimes is difficult to recognise. It is hardly surprising that there is resistance to committing to such unspectacular service work. Everyone prefers a more important, more visible role, and the admiration and applause which go with it. Life in a monastery is in essence a life of service. We forget that in its original and proper sense, being a superior is a service. Although outwardly it seems that it mainly brings accolade, taking up this task means in fact taking on much difficulty, responsibility and stress. It is always service in the space of encounters – creating the opportunity for contact and ensuring the right conditions for it.

Let us pause for a moment on the final fragment of *Mazurka in C major* op. 56 No. 2. We clearly hear there two melodic lines imitating each other. They are in a transparent, strongly delineated relationship of dialogue. In order to maintain it, or perhaps give it full expression, it is necessary to add a harmonic complement. Discreetly present, it appears as the right space for that dialogue.

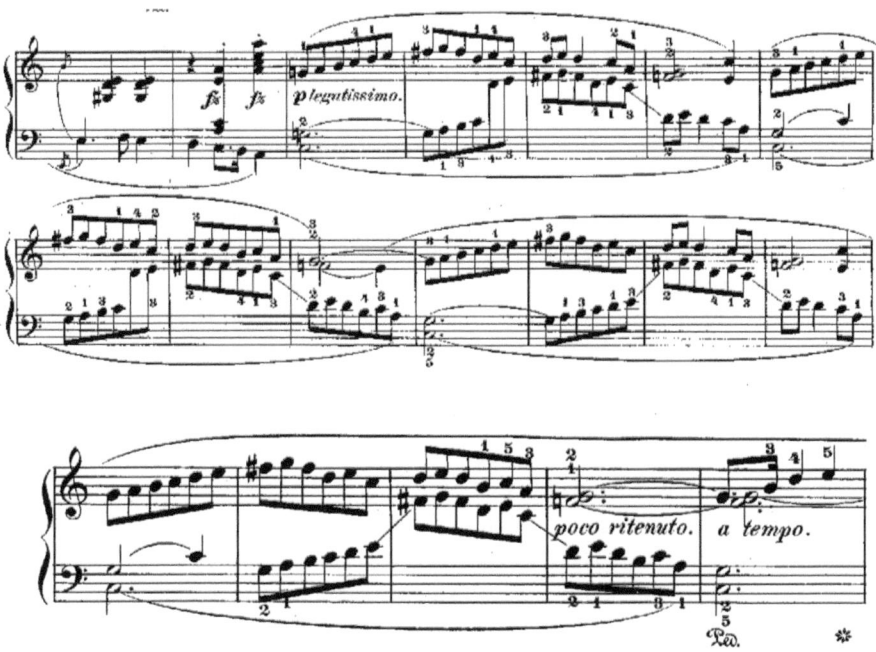

Our functioning often looks like this. We owe much to people whose care subtly, almost imperceptibly, creates a proper and safe framework for that event or another, serving to ensure the right atmosphere for an encounter or dialogue, for understanding and acceptance. Such people are a treasure in a team. Yet their effort is patient and humble, sometimes difficult to notice. They work through seemingly minor gestures, a few words that turn out to be important. It is in this ordinary way that an atmosphere of trust, mutual good will and love is created. We can interpret in a similar manner the examples of Chopin's polyphony quoted above.

Life with others truly feeds on variety. It is thanks to the otherness of those we encounter that it takes on colour and taste. In many cases this is equivalent to undertaking difficult contacts and relationships. To accept another person means to accept that person's otherness. Meeting them means stepping forward to meet their otherness half way. There is no other way of forming relationships. That is a great challenge, but also an opportunity for the contemporary world. More and more often various nationalities, traditions or cultures, want to, or are forced to, live together in one place. This is what happens in, for example, Bolzano, a Swiss town where three languages – and thus three cultures – German, Italian and Retro Romanisch coexist together. This is not easy and – taking into account even such issues as legal or institutional arrangements – costs a great deal. However, maintaining a delicate balance in this area is very worthwhile, if only because of the rich variety which becomes available through it. This is a situation which increasingly applies throughout Europe. The multitude and variety of immigrants means a diversity of mentalities, sensitivities, customs and traditions. Undoubtedly this is always a potential area of conflict. However, it is very important to undertake small, local attempts at making such a complex reality work. They may turn out to be a useful laboratory for coming up with new standards and qualities of a fruitful life together. Fortunately, it is very often the case that at the lowest levels – the practical ones, sometimes everyday ones – contacts between groups or communities which fundamentally (and officially) are enemies are not quite so bad. Meetings, or even cooperation, do take place. This is an example of a kind of "musicality" towards another person, a sensitivity to polyphony, whose nature requires otherness, but one that is open and ready for dialogue.

We have mentioned the fact that the use of polyphony is possible owing to the adoption of certain principles. Often their very possibility awakens mistrust and fear. Our freedom seems to be threatened. In practice, however, it turns out that these principles are not at all terrible. With good will and sensitivity they seem to come to mind naturally. Of course, one needs some skill and experience. However, the most important things are good will and sincere intentions. If we think too much, analyse too much or attach ideology to one or another reality – the attitude or behaviour of other people, the potential danger they represent – this may cause much damage to the authenticity and fruitfulness of the relationship. Openness and sincerity do not do away with risk in a relationship, but they are, to a degree, a condition of minimising, or even avoiding it. It is only in this way that we can be ourselves and achieve further development.

Let the conclusion to the above remarks be provided by an analysis, and a hearing, of *Nocturne in E-flat major* op. 55 No. 2. This is another unusual nocturne, an infrequent – for Chopin – example of a uniform treatment of this genre: we do not find here contrasting, clearly distinguishable parts; the narration flows as one stream; yes, it is nuanced, but maintains the same intensity of expression. This work has the character of a single dialogue, a conversation taking place in an atmosphere of closeness, attention and concern. The two upper voices delineate the two melodic lines conducting the dialogue. They interweave, complement each other, result from each other. All this takes place in a singular climate of sophisticated and eager delicacy, a calm full of care and tenderness, constantly provided by the line of accompaniment entrusted to the lowest voice. Systematically and unfailingly, always with the appropriate flexibility, it provides the harmonic base for the dialogue of the two highest voices. They provide a moving illustration of a clear and deep relationship, not free from tensions but always capable of their creative integration. It is an illustration of a dialogue of two different partners who are open and sensitive to each other, always seeking opportunities or ways of complementing each other, or, rather, of mutual help. The two highest voices accompany each other, intertwine with great patience and good will, providing a moving example of a full life in peace and harmony. Some commentators describe this nocturne as a musical illustration of a dialogue between two people in love. Let this comment provide a beautiful conclusion of our description of this work. (*Nocturne in E-flat major op. 55 No. 2)

The Others – Patience and Consistency

Halfway through these deliberations, a few words about patience. In chapter 7 of his *Rule*, St Benedict describes the twelve degrees of humility. It is a spiritual path the undertaking of which is bound to help a monk in putting the instructions of the *Rule* into practice. If he travels all the way, he will achieve the aim of his life: salvation. Much could be thought and said on the subject of that proposal of St Benedict, through examining the meaning and the sequence of these degrees. Some of them are, perhaps, easier to achieve, others are more difficult. Practical life tests theoretical guidelines very thoroughly. Without analysing all the twelve degrees of humility, it is perhaps worth mentioning just one of them, the one that might be the most difficult. In any case, in today's reality this is the one which might meet the greatest resistance, making it difficult, if not impossible, to break out of the purely human thinking and argumentation, and be led by St Benedict to what is everlasting and supranatural.

> *The fourth degree of humility is, that, if hard and distasteful things are commanded, nay, even though injuries are inflicted, he accept them with patience and even temper, and not grow weary or give up, but hold out, as the Scripture saith: "He that shall persevere unto the end shall be saved" (Mt 10:22). And again: "Let thy heart take courage, and wait thou for the Lord" (Ps 26[27]:14). And showing that a faithful man ought even to bear every disagreeable thing for the Lord, it saith in the person of the suffering: "For Thy sake we suffer death all the day long; we are counted as sheep for the slaughter" (Rom 8:36; Ps 43[44]:22). (RulBen 7, 43–49).*

Today, when our need for a comfortable existence is perhaps greater than ever before, it is hardly surprising that we try to ensure it in every possible way. Thus, we organise the conditions and the environment in which we have to function in a way that best suits our preferences. Things get worse when our comfort conflicts with someone else's or when, in order to carry out some task, we have to give it up. It sometimes happens that, when choosing between our good and the good of the "cause", we choose our own benefit. We thus refuse to carry out this or that task, justifying it, of course, in various ways. But usually we are simply defending our comfort. In the view of the monastic tradition – in the view of St Benedict – such situations may take on the character of the Paschal way, at least in an embryonic form.

That is, of course, if we decide to do it, accepting the effort of giving up our own comfort. But is this not the fundamental condition of imitating Jesus Christ, as the Gospels tell us to do? Here opens a space for long-term work on oneself.

Its weak point is breaking in our own will – which, looking at it another way, is the constant motif of classical asceticism. Speaking more plainly, what may be concerned may even be living against one's own preferences.

Here, patience turns out to be merely the point of departure. Tolerance towards others who often stand in our way is also not sufficient. What is needed is an active and constructive attitude, particularly when one has to carry out some task, to implement some project – and to do it in spite of everything. What becomes necessary then is not just to overcome this or that obstacle, but simple perseverance. Patience and good intentions are best tested in just such situations. They enter directly into service of the order, and through it (and thus indrectly), of the freedom and the wide perspective of the course of the melody. This is necessary in order to provide a feeling of confidence, peace and security in the face of the lack of restraint that a melody enjoys. St Benedict opens up clear and positive prospects to those who are patient:

> *And secure in the hope of the divine reward, they go on joyfully, saying: "But in all these things we overcome because of Him that hath loved us" (Rom 8:37).*

(RulBen 7, 49–50). This is because patience is needed in very many situations in our life: patience towards others, towards ourselves, when making plans and implementing them, when we encounter obstacles and when we overcome them.

A good analogy for this kind of challenge is the process of preparing a musical composition for presentation or recording. How much patience is needed for this! Many hours, days and weeks of repetition of the same fragments, phrases, go into preparing a given work for a presentation that will last a few shorter or longer moments. And yet, a momentary lack of attention may destroy even something prepared with so much effort. Of course, these days the problems of recording are somewhat less acute, but the precision and the ruthlessness of a phonographic record causes stress of a different kind. In both cases, alongside determination and patience, one needs humility and alertness. Behind all this, of course, there must be strong motivation – why do I want to play? Why do I choose this composition and not another? To whom do I want to present it? What do I want to express in my performance? All these questions do not just testify to a sense of responsibility. They are the basis of any conscious activity to which we want to impart the fullest possible meaning. They need to be asked whenever we undertake any task that is important to us and requires our commitment. That approach is very close to that of St Benedict, being also very evangelical. It is enough to look at the eighth chapter of St John's Gospel, or the story of the meeting on the road to Emmaus between Jesus and the disciples (Luke 24,13–35). There is so much sensitivity, patience, humility, penetration, consistency and courage there! The most important point of the reality in which these scenes take place has been aimed at, and touched to perfection. Something important is happening there. External events lead onward and inward. To make this possible, it is necessary to have distance and concentration, a clear vision of the goal and the effect of our actions, as well as perfect knowledge of the circumstances surrounding the event. That which is less important, which belongs in the background, should be clearly separated from that which is significant. And with all of that goes effort – the effort of constant leaving, returning, taking up again, testing, correcting, constant checking of the ultimate prospect. It is, in a sense, a breaking down into components of the existential "going out from self" and "returning to self", as described by Heidegger; not only in order to understand and make better use of one's potential, but also to get to know better the external circumstances which condition our activities.

Movement of this kind must be present if we live and function in any human community. The individual has to constantly keep leaving his or her safe position, move towards the others, whether s/he wants to or not, confronting them – in order to return "to oneself" a moment later. The outside, the motion towards activity has to keep being balanced by a return to base, to the inside, to the depths. This is the existential justification of the Benedictine device *ora et labora*, but this is also the permanent context of all our relationships with others and our functioning in the world. Without support, without an awareness of the meaning, it is difficult to see any project through with consistency. The external "resistance of matter" naturally blocks all that which wants to be created.

On a number of occasions Chopin used a clear, basic "leading thought" – a motif from which the whole work develops – in the structure and form of his compositions. Of course, history of music is familiar with this type of compositional technique (as, for example, such variational forms as passacaglia, chaconne or folia). What is special about Chopin is the particular dialectic of that motif with the other musical matter, which results from it but at times is opposed to it. It is difficult not to see here an analogy to the basic existential situation described above. Chopin's sensitivity and musical "honesty" allowed him, in a penetrating manner, to shape his music on a number of occasions. We can hear it quite often in the etudes, preludes and mazurkas. Basically, however, the embryonic motif, discreet and servant-like, integrates itself into the whole of a higher order, without great expressive significance. It signalises something at the beginning. It proposes a certain expressive quality – and immediately dissolves itself into the greater whole. However, in *Etude in A minor* op. 25 No. 11 what happens is a little different. At the beginning we have a simple and clearly defined motif – almost purely rhythmical.

After its repetition, like an echo, although a harmonised one, there appears a cascade of the actual sound material of that etude: rich figurations played by the right hand. The motif accompanies them as a constant point of reference, or even a special kind of counterpoint. A certain obsessiveness in its repetition imparts to the whole etude a very expressive, not to say dramatic, character. Finally, it seems as if everything reduces to that motif, although it appears insignificant against the figurations it juxtaposes. It dominates through a structure that is more extended than itself – or, simply, provides a point of departure for it. (* *Etude in A minor* op. 25 No. 11)

A relationship between an individual element and the greater whole which grows out of it appears wherever we as individuals, in one way or another, confront a group of people, a community. We can give something of ourselves, we can exert influence – or we can simply melt into it almost without a trace. Our relationship with a group usually begins from our appearing "on the outside", after which we make an attempt to get closer and enter the group – or we walk away from it. We can then follow the trail, the influences which we leave on the group. Do we enter into the centre of it, into its heart, become decision-makers – or do we place ourselves somewhere at the side? Bipolarity of this kind, but also possessed of constant dynamism, becomes the principle of *Etude in A minor* discussed above. The whole composition is constructed around the initial motif. In spite of the expressive development of its discourse – progressions, transpositions, dynamic changes, modulations – we keep on hearing the same motif, although in different configurations. Chopin was not the first to have this idea. Probably this kind of construction principle comes from instrumental music, where a particular arrangement of the hand and the range of movements related to it translate into specific soud motifs. A classic example of such a work is *Prelude in C major* from the first volume of *Das wohltemperierte Klavier* by Johann Sebastian Bach, on which Charles Gounod based the melody of his famous *Ave Maria*. Simplicity, compactness and transparency of music shaped in this way is made possible only because of the consistency and discipline in the treatment of the material. A motif, once chosen, must "last" until the end. Thus it is important to choose well, and then to limit oneself to being faithful to it. The greater the patience and the consistency, the clearer and stronger the final effect.

Is there not in this music, full of daring, a space created for freedom and grace? Its daring seems to oppose the limitedness of the basic motif, yet this opposition only increases the expressive tension. It is not easy to implement an idea. Usually at the very beginning it is very unimpressive, it is difficult to expect it to come to something. And yet the determination and the dynamism it hides may cause it to be realised, and that undoubtedly must cost much. The effort does not involve just patience and consistency. One also needs imagination to see the final shape of the idea when it is realised, the faith that it is possible, as well as the skill of overcoming the difficulties which appear on the way. It is a kind of struggle, but also a fascinating adventure in creativity. That is how, from a small embryo, emerges a large, complex construction. And such situations happen in our lives many times. Through meagre means we are supposed to achieve – and we do achieve – quite significant goals. That is how the masterpieces of the human spirit are created, always because of what might be termed "obsession", patience, perseverance. The road to them bears clear marks of the Way of the Cross. This is the best and most accessible ascetic practice. People often make up their own imaginary problems, or exercise abstract virtues based on their own whim. Yet a concrete task, undertaken and carried out in a concrete context, is the best test of the quality of our humanity. Reliability, faithfulness, responsibility are best practised and tested in just this way, accepting and overcoming with humility the difficulties which stand in our way. This does mean that life seems to be spent in a state of constant confrontation, but it is then rich in the potential of new qualities.

The evangelical model of such an attitude is clearly woven through the consecutive pages of St Benedict's *Rule*. It is only by adopting it that one can guarantee the clear and unequivocal stance of a monk – faithfulness, constancy and fruitfulness of life. According to Ovid's famous adage, dripping water hollows out stone not by its force but by constant perseverance. One can achieve most not by violent or aggressive activity, but sometimes by taking it slowly, surrendering to the "monotony" of patience. Such a style of action is fundamental to monastic life – ordinary, orderly and systematic. It is a life not of great bursts, but constant movement forward – one might say, of "hollowing out" of subjects or matters. It is thus not surprising that we now need to refer to one of Chopin's best known works, *Prelude in D-flat major* op. 28 No. 15. It is described as the "raindrop" prelude, undoubtedly because of the obsessive repetition of the same, single note, the dominant A flat. Throughout, we can hear the main line of the melody and the accompaniment, but the repeated note seems to penetrate the tissue of the whole work, being most apparent in pauses and on the boundaries of phrases, like raindrops falling constantly – in the background, but soaking through everything. On the basis of this obsession Chopin composed a larger form, as if accepting the experience of obsession and making it constructive by developing it and integrating it into a larger whole. What seemed destructive thus gains a positive, constructive dimension. (**Prelude in D-flat major* op. 28 No. 15)

Like the rain of our grey everyday reality, our servitude and humiliations, the rituals, the prayers, the meals, our departures and returns, our encounters with people that we repeat constantly – we are accompanied by obsessive repeatability, made up of the gestures and events of our life. And yet it is out of these that we are supposed to construct its shape, visible in its totality on the outside – not just that, but a life that is meant to leave its mark on the surrounding reality, to be our legacy when we are gone. Constantly taking up anew that which is the same – that is the singular privilege of Benedictine life. Benedictine identity seems to be woven from many levels of repeatability – daily, weekly and yearly rhythm of liturgy, assemblies of the community, periods of silence and conversation, work and rest. However, observing the world carefully we may be amazed how much patience, perseverance and consistency there is in it – not just in nature but in many human activities which, indeed, serve all of us: information, development of technology, but also catering or transport. What motivates millions of people to constant concentration and unweakening effort? To win against competition, the desire to be the best, to achieve the greatest possible profit. These are the reasons why people not only expend their energies, but acquire neuroses, sometimes destroying their health. So much commitment to gain what is only material and fleeting. And what about matters and values of greatest importance? What about loyalty to another person, to oneself, about love, hope? This concerns consequences that are not tangible, cannot be tested by touch. And yet so often we seem to brush against that which is eternal. It is so close – and at the same time so far away! We often lack motivation, strength – we fall down exhausted, lacking hope, in despair. We want to run away from life into dreams. Or life itself seems to us like a dream, sometimes very much like a nightmare. Here is *Berceuse*, Chopin's lullaby: a little like a contemplation, a meditation on human fate. The obsessiveness of our struggles is sublimated here into a sophisticated construction, a cycle of variations based on the same, simple but constantly repeated motif played by the left hand which at the same time opens the whole composition. On the series of its repetition is superimposed a melody which develops in an increasingly exquisite way within the space of the texture and ornamentation. This increases the embryonic contrast between the repeated motif of the accompaniment and the wide, richly developed melodic line, as if testifying to the thesis that a truly interesting, beautiful and developing life is possible thanks to the regularity, monotony, or even obsession hidden in its depths. This is a contrast not only to be observed but to be discovered in our everyday life. (**Berceuse in D-flat major* op. 57)

This work can also be viewed in another way. It is, in a sense, a testimony to faithfulness in love or, more precisely, the search for contact with the beloved person, constantly attempting to say anew that which is most important and, finally, constantly maintaining a living contact in spite of the changes in the other person. The ongoing dialectic tension between that which is unchanging and the various forms in which it is realised is, indeed, a deep axis of that which is always happening between us and other people.

The Yearning

Let us take Chopin's first opused nocturne, *Nocturne in B minor* op. 9 No. 1, as the "motto" of the fragment of these deliberations devoted to the subject of yearning. It is one of his first compositions of this kind. What is amazing and moving here, from the very beginning, is the character of the very clearly introduced melody, simple but strangely yearning, or even sad. It is puzzling that it should have come from the pen of a composer who was quite young, a musical genius who (at least theoretically) was standing at the gates to a beautiful life. Perhaps it would be going too far to suggest that the nature of this melody might have been a presentiment of the composer's difficult, and in its own way dramatic, fate. And yet one talks about Chopin's regret! What draws attention is the great expressive power of the initial motif of this nocturne. From it grows the further course of the first part of the work; the musical material which appears later no longer contains such an expressive charge, as if, humbly, it did not dare compete with the melody which begins the nocturne. Let us try to enter deeper into this initial melody, or rather into the space which it opens: what feelings, what images accompany us as we listen? Does its sadness carry peace or depression? Is it not the case that it carries a certain nobility, discretion, almost timidity, and yet directness, simplicity and sincerity? (**Nocturne in B minor* op. 9 No.1)

To return to the evangelical archetype of the *Rule* of St Benedict, we think of the sadness of Jesus: his seriousness, his restraint and his tears. In the Gospels we find more descriptions of Jesus's sad moments than happy ones. This does not mean that Jesus did not experience joy – he did, and did so in a variety of ways, but the most affecting marks were left on Him, and on us as well, by those telling and moving moments of His sadness. Why is it so? Perhaps "being suspended" between heaven and earth – the fate of Man-God – in itself is more deserving of tears than a smile (of course, as far as it is possible to think like this within our categories of knowing and understanding the Mystery of God). And yet one cannot remain indifferent to the claim, both concise and strong: *My soul is sorrowful even unto death* (Mark 14,34). It is hardly surprising that St Benedict is very restrained where laughter is concerned in his *Rule*. He advocates monks "not to love much or boisterous laughter." (RulBen 4,55), but here also it is not a matter of total rejection of joy. Any emotional colouring, both in the Gospels and in St Benedict's *Rule*, must ultimately be interpreted within the Paschal perspective. The words from the chapter *On the keeping of Lent* are both thought-provoking and very clear in this respect. They recommend to a monk that he should "with the gladness of spiritual desire await holy Easter" (ibid., 49, 6). Joy is combined here, as if directly and automatically, with yearning. The Latin original conveys this link even more precisely: *cum spiritualis desiderii gaudio*. The categories of sadness and joy in the message of the gospels are linked, both in their diachronic (after sadness on earth there will be joy in heaven) and synchronic dimensions (every earthly joy has some sadness in it; as we say, "there is no rose without thorns"). In both cases perhaps we should be talking about "laughter through tears". Perhaps only such joy is true and trustworthy, and has a chance to become salt of the earth? The fragile yet certain joy of Easter morning only becomes possible after the tragedy of Easter Friday and the gnawing emptiness, as well as the longing of Easter Saturday. Our search for total happiness and joy is destined to be filled with yearning and sadness. Perhaps, however, this is the only way in which it can maintain its dynamism…? Our striving for happiness would thus be equivalent to searching within ourselves for traces of the yearning and the care of God – which appears to be closely akin to the experience of Chopin, a disconsolate soul conscious of its mission but finally ground down by the impossibility of fulfilling it to perfection. Exile, the longing for the homeland, a feeling of helplessness in the face of destiny, these are the main areas of Chopin's lack of fulfilment. If we add to it the growing health problems, as well as a perfectionist attitude to his own work, the panorama of this lack of fulfilment undoubtedly extends proportionately to the sensitivity which, as we know, was very much a part of Chopin's character. It is difficult to say whether the inclination of his temperament was superimposed on this. It gives one pause for thought that Chopin's first composition, still recorded by his teacher, Wojciech Żywny, rather than himself, is in the tonality of G minor and contains an admixture of the melancholy described above. The work in question, *Polonaise in G minor*, composed by the seven-year-old Chopin, integrates this melancholy into the correctly perceived classical elegance. Everything remains transparent, open – yet conscious of lack of fulfilment. (**Polonaise in G minor*)

Again, the question arises – whence that sad contemplation? In fact, we find it in young Chopin's other early works composed in Warsaw: in his first opused mazurka (*Mazurka in F-sharp minor* op. 6 No. 1) (**Mazurka in F-sharp minor* op. 6 No. 1), as well as in the third nocturne from the first nocturne opus (*Nocturne in B major* op. 9 No. 3). It is significant that the latter work, in spite of its tonality being major, acquires that nostalgic colouring, so characteristic of all Chopin's later works, through the chromatisation clearly present in the main motif. (**Nocturne in B major* op. 9 No. 3)

The question about the reasons for such a sad and nostalgic stylistic profile remains relevant and open. Regardless of the possibility, or justification, for an answer to it, it seems beyond doubt that Chopin's nostalgia gathers and expresses an important aspect of not just the Polish soul. Far ideals, looked to and hoped for, once familiar and now lost and beyond reach yet needed so very much: that is the essence of what we are trying to express now, and that is such an important aspect of Chopin's expression and its mystery. There are in it, in equal measure, the longing and the experience of one's own fragility and helplessness; looking far forward and struggling with one's own unhealed loneliness.

At this point we reach another puzzling but significant dimension of the kinship between Chopin's music and the Benedictine tradition. It is the experience of loneliness, taken up in the perspective of yearning. Such a struggle is probably known to anyone who tries to stay faithful to the priorities which they recognise, yet experiences obstacles and lack of understanding from others. It is a humble acceptance of a difficult fate without abandoning the memory of ideals. Our sadness is very often the result of many disappointments. Projects which could not be realised, other people, incomprehensible and unpleasant situations, difficult choices, unforeseen consequences of various decisions, missed opportunities which cannot be retrieved. There is in all this a Proustian awareness of time irrevocably lost. But perhaps it is simply a permanent element of human fate – the constant challenge of living with the yearning, or rather, in spite of it? The greatness and beauty of Chopin's music consists in the fact that even when it expresses that sadness or yearning, it also brings comfort and hope. They come not only from the awareness that someone before us had to cope with such powerful longing. They are part of the way that Chopin conveys sadness through his music. There is much discretion there, restraint in spite of everything, even elegance, nobility and dignity. It is not a display of pain, or cheap sentimentality, so frequent in Romanticism. When we listen to Chopin we are dealing with what seems more like embarrassment, even shamefacedness, at times even with a "silent cry". His music touches the yearning, or perhaps, rather, directs towards it, but does not itself become the yearning. It seems to gather it, and to express it in our name, but at the same time it shows its ultimate perspective – somewhere beyond this earthly life, beyond the horizon of our limitations. And yearning experienced in this way becomes a way of opening ourselves – a space of hope, an opportunity to entrust ourselves to a loving person, to God. It is not strange, then, that Chopin's music feels so intimate. It brings a sense of closeness; it imparts a feeling of solidarity, understanding, even though pain remains pain and yearning remains yearning. Like a tear that does not really change anything and yet seems to help, to move the pain forward. We thus need to take care of the "smile through tears"

When one of the monks, a year after obtaining his doctorate, was elected abbot by his fellow brethren, he was given by his supervisor two postcards with reproductions of pictures by Picasso. One showed a clown preparing for a show: already wearing the appropriate costume, he intrigues by the tinge of sadness on his face. Yes, it is a result of concentration, as well as uncertainty and loneliness. Hands, clenched as if in readiness for the performance, emphasise further this feeling of helplessness. And on the other postcard, an old clown gives his advice to a younger one. Both are partly dressed in circus costumes (or the remains of them), both have an expression of sadness on their faces, and face each his own way. Two lonelinesses touching and supporting each other. In another way, this is an eloquent illustration of our situation in today's world, where we have to perform in a spectacle in which we perhaps do not fit well, often putting on a brave face when playing a difficult game. Understanding is not always forthcoming, one remains somewhere deep in one's loneliness. The world goes its own way. We do not have much influence on the part we are destined to play, and yet we have to give it our all. The result is most often beyond our reach. You have to endure, in spite of the tears welling up in your eyes, or perhaps even after the tears have dried up. In the monastic tradition this is the attitude described as *apatheia* – resistance to all external stimuli, "immovability", peace. In a sense this is the character of Chopin's music itself. We talked about it being discreet; its objectivity, perhaps better described as serviceability, is also worthy of note. Without focusing attention on itself, it tries to transmit something more than itself. It wants to be "played back" in the hearts and souls of its listeners, although its effect remains beyond it. Giving all of itself, it no longer expects anything – and does not need anything. What follows is no longer its concern. The part of a monk should also be understood in terms of such categories, particularly in today's world. Indeed, it may be intriguing, old-fashioned for some, weird at best: the clothes, the rituals, the limitations – they do not help in creating a positive reception of monasticism in modern society. Let us remember, however, that from the very beginning of their existence, i.e., the turn of the third and fourth centuries A.D., monks had no ambition of becoming "somebodies". They simply wanted to live for God, in an ordinary way, concentrating on what is essential and most significant. Usually, however, what happened was that, unintentionally, such an "ordinary" lifestyle drew people and aroused their curiosity. And so it remains to this day: the aura of monasteries and the behaviours linked to them continue to act as an invitation to stop surfing over the contemporary standards and to ask oneself certain questions. The life of a monk is thus – or rather should be – like a melody, in itself discreet, providing a service, yet sufficiently distinct and appealing to attract and draw to itself and thus towards something more distant, towards greater depths. It is, in a sense, the reality of a spectacle, a stage performance, with all the tension and potential that that contains. It is along these lines that we should interpret the painting by the French painter Rouault, which represents Christ as a clown. It is a telling symbol of the status of values in today's world; not just Christian values, but everything which somewhere, in the distance, perhaps the ultimate distance, in some way involves a reference to Jesus Christ. As we said before, you do indeed need courage, consistency and perseverance, but the initial condition to be met is a kind of enchantment, a rapture, an uncompromising entry into an area of unequivocal simplicity. The power of that consists in that which is obvious and most important, because it is closest to our heart. At the same time, because of the presence of others and because of external circumstances, it must become an area of confrontation, a "sign of opposition" which carries pain and a threat of rejection. In an era of constant pressure of images, information and media, maintaining an attitude like this is almost impossible, as is maintaining the purity and authenticity of Chopin's melodic line in a world of ubiquituous commerce and enormous technical possibilities. Everyone who has, at least once, experienced and deeply felt the unearthly beauty of the delicate line of Chopin's cantilena, carries a responsibility for this unique space of encounter, the unique form of contact with the inner world of another. It is a mission, an urgent necessity of sharing a gift that is inexpressible and yet explains so much.

That is why constant sensitivity to this melody line, a steadfast concern for its existence, its shape, its fate, is so important. Who knows, perhaps this is the very essence of yearning: the awareness that that which is most important and most beautiful is at the same time so delicate and so fragile; the knowledge that we cannot control it to the full, and that, to an extent, it has to be subjected to a variety of threats. What remains is an inexplicable trust that all will be well – in spite of everything. Yet this is the very entanglement of sadness and hope, the "purest *apatheia*", the essence of true longing. There is nothing here that we might lose; we have been given everything. That which is important and valuable – is grace.

A monk, fast approaching the threshold of death, confessed to his abbot that his greatest effort was devoted to fighting attacks of sadness. This was nothing to do with depression, but probably everything to do with the awareness of his helplessness in the face of the realities of life and the fate of his ideals. Who among us has not experienced this, sooner or later, in one form or another? Music has always been man's faithful – perhaps most faithful – companion in such struggles. Who knows, perhaps it was even born out of yearning…? Many traces of that yearning can be found in the Gregorian chant. Within eight tones, in many of them it creates a space full of longing and melancholy, using the simplest of all possible means, a system of semitones, the character of the melodic motion. That, however, is a separate subject which can only be acknowledged here. Let us note only that Chopin's "nostalgia" is largely linked to the manner of leading the melodic line. As in the Gregorian chant, the constant play, the dialectic of semitones, their interweaving with whole tones and filling larger intervals with them, play an enormous part in shaping the profile of that line. Perhaps that measure of sadness or longing written and heard in music shows how close music is to humankind? Acceptance also of sadness with humility and courage, perceiving hope in it, is, in some degree, a way of being faithful to the Paschal way of Jesus Christ.

It would be impossible to end these reflections without referring to their emblematic composition, *Etude in E major* op. 10 No. 3, sometimes described as "Sadness" (*La tristesse*). Apparently Chopin described the melody which opens this work, its main motif, as the most beautiful he had ever written. Again, as in the case of the early opuses referred to previously, the feeling of regret and sadness breaks through the major tonality. To what extent this is due to being contradictory, or to the composer's lack of control over his mood of sadness that "flows over", perhaps, something one does not need to know. An important role in the "yearning" development in this melody is undoubtedly played by semitones, but also by the character of the melodic movement, as if cautious, uncertain, developing in small steps. One is struck by the strong contrast introduced by the middle part of the etude, what almost amounts to an explosion of violent expressiveness. One has the impression that the sadness has to break into spasms, into something like outbursts of passion. But is this not what happens in ordinary life? Let each of us answer that question for ourselves. What is important is the suggestiveness of the experiences, or rather their trustworthiness. Sadness appears to us more believable than joy. *Etude in E major* tries to combine them into one, a singular expressive experience. It may not be powerful, but it is undoubtedly very close to our human affairs, and thus perennially moving, as if dedicated to those who are afraid of trusting acceptance of the yearning, and of entering it with hope. (*Etude in E major op. 10 No. 3)

Emotions

Feelings, or emotions, are understood here in the classical sense, as the internal motions of our spirit, and something which often escapes our control. They are often an expression of some contradiction hidden within us, which paradoxically acquires the characteristics of a dynamism impossible to ignore. It is therefore difficult, if not impossible, to give an unequivocal answer to the question about its origin and its causes. This is because here we brush against our "other self', our second nature, one which most frequently surprises ourselves and, if not simply embarrassing, might perhaps be even shameful. Psychology, or psychoanalysis, try to describe feelings in a variety of ways, attempting to find out how far they reflect the attitudes which we suppress and how far they are part of our nature. The matter of their identity and character is also a question about pain, fear, joy, envy, i.e., the states of our psyche which colour and determine our everyday reality to the greatest degree. They are something which we can examine as if from the outside, which we can try to control, evaluate, perhaps even shape. When we live through them, we experience very strongly our limitedness and fragility – or, simply, the truth about our human condition.

Chopin, as an artist, must undoubtedly have been particularly susceptible to feelings. His music, but perhaps also his personality, not only "fed" off them, but must have allowed them to be displayed, to become their expression. However, it would be a mistake to describe Chopin's music as emotional. He himself was always on guard against the danger of falling into cheap emotionalism, and found the literal expression of feelings distasteful. It was for this reason that he attached such great importance to form, which in his work became an important component of expression. In this, his models were undoubtedly Mozart and J.S. Bach, whom he regarded particularly highly. In Chopin's case we are thus dealing with music that is highly organised. Everything is planned, and carefully measured out. Paradoxically, this allows a much wider horizon of expressiveness – one might say, its development on the macroscale, which ultimately brings a much stronger and enduring effect than moving only within the smaller area of the microscale, i.e., at the level of the play of motifs, within the range of short temporal units. However, on occasion emotions seem to escape Chopin's control, pouring out as a clear and violent stream, and he himself was aware of it. This concerns primarily compositions written at a time which was difficult for him, immediately after leaving his homeland, when, having parted from those closest to him, he received the disturbing news of the beginning of the November 1830 uprising. Chopin himself confessed that he was "thundering on the piano"[12], and traces of this can be found in the outlying parts of *Scherzo in B minor* op. 20 (**Scherzo in B minor* op. 20), as well as some preludes and etudes, such as the two in C minor, the last ones from opuses 10 and 25. (* *Etude in C minor* op. 10 No. 12)

Feelings, particularly intense and violent ones, evoke questions about their causes. In the case of music, an explanation may be provided by the title or biographical circumstances which accompany the creation of a given work. Feelings, however, want to share themselves with other people. Their expression not only helps the composer, but often provides the impetus for the creation of a work. This also has a social dimension, becoming a sign of solidarity or even comfort, since we recognise our own experiences in the feelings expressed by art. We can get to understand them better, but we can also try to cope with them better. Although every feeling is experienced in a unique and individual manner, one can presumably distinguish certain groups within them – or find in them, as has been said at the beginning of these deliberations, particular modules. Bearing in mind what has been written in relation to Chopin's sadness, it is not difficult to describe the main lines of expression, and thus the feelings expressed in Chopin's music. The yearning and the sadness are accompanied by sometimes heroic rebellion against the political and historical situation of Poland of that time. It is combined with a feeling of powerlessness, or even despair. There is an embarrassment, a helplessness – but also great power, which made Schumann describe Chopin's music as "cannons buried in flowers". Truly, emotions are a great force, on condition that they find the right form through which they can make their effect felt. Properly managed and organised (and thus subjected to something which seems to be against their nature), they become a force which does not pass without leaving its impression. This paradox of "organising," of "taming" emotions in order to display them as clearly as possible, is something that appears naturally in the music of the greatest masters, with Mozart in the forefront. Chopin, who admired Mozart, expressed emotions in his music in precisely this, "organised", one might say "Mozartian" way, in the majority of his compositions. Elegance and restraint, even laconicism, go together here with great precision and awareness of form. Emotion here is not so much – or not only – the cause of this and not another sound construction: it is also intended to be the fruit of hearing this construction. There is a sophistication here, at times even perverseness. How

---

12   *Korespondencja*, I, p. 162. Letter from Vienna dated 26 December 1830 to Jan Matuszyński.

is one to control one's emotions, to plan and organise their transmission, when they tear at one mercilessly on all sides? Perhaps the greatness of the Romantic genius, the demiurge who creates a perfectly shaped work out of the elemental emotions, consists in that? And in the case of Chopin, as we have already said, the matters which were usually involved were of the greatest importance, both vital and dramatic. The problem is that our times, today, are so swollen with emotions that the diapason of their expressions seems to reach its peak and the threshold of our sensitivity to them must keep moving upwards. It is thus difficult for us today to feel the original scale of expressiveness contained in Chopin's works at the time when they were created. Some matters, at one time important and dramatic, perhaps do not affect us to the same degree today. But important things seem to be carriers of emotions that are always strong. The only clear-cut example of Jesus's anger, recorded in the second chapter of St John's Gospel, concerns the most important matter: the glory of the House of the Father! However, it is also true that our emotional reactions very often are not adequate to their cause. It is only by being aware of this that we can effectively test our emotions, make them trustworthy. And this leads us back to the question we asked before: what really hides behind a given emotion? Does the form of its expression fit the importance of the cause? Adequate, convincing emotions are an expression of a person's maturity. Their right expression testifies to the artist's sense of responsibility. Chopin's music provides many examples of precisely such working through and displaying of emotions: their intensity and effect work as powerfully on us today. Most frequently these emotions concerned national themes, expressing the painful and dramatic experiences of a nation struggling with the loss of its independence. However, written into this is Chopin's personal drama – the whole range of his own longings and lack of fulfilment. As we mentioned earlier, his greatness consists in the extraordinary combination of the personal with the general. It is for this reason, that he was able to transmit successfully the experiences of many of his countrymen, in a sense making them his own, while at the same time engaging his talent in the service of the "Holiest Cause". An example of this kind of expressiveness is *Polonaise in F-sharp minor* op. 44 – a composition with a wide, expansive form and distinct narration, not devoid of pathos. From the very beginning, which presents a decisive and clearly delineated theme, we become aware of enormous determination and emotionality. The melody, developed consistently, time after time takes on an almost "spasmodic" character. At times the motifs are repeated, as if they had to overcome some resistance. The rich texture of the dense chords imparts to this dynamic music both seriousness and vigour. (**Polonaise in F-sharp minor* op. 44)

In this way great emotions express a great drama, as well as a great yearning for freedom and justice. One might get the impression that the ultimate means have been employed here. Chopin throws onto the scales his elegance and his restraint, which almost seemed strained. This is what happens in our life, when in a relationship with another we have exhausted all the available means, and the only thing left to us is to involve our emotions. Usually this comes at a high cost, but if we do it skilfully we might achieve an effect. It is well known that a confrontation of this kind carries a risk of upsetting someone, even of conflict. The emotion becomes a form of energy which can be employed in all kinds of causes. We know it only too well from experience. On the one hand, such actions are usually extreme; on the other, we need to learn how to tame and manage the energy of our feelings. In any kind of pursuit, they may turn out to be a valuable, perhaps irreplaceable, tool, enlivening our motivation and activity.

What is interesting is that in St Benedict's *Rule* this dynamism of feelings is often recalled by diverse uses of words related to the verbs "to desire" (*desiderare*) and "to want" (*volere*)[13]. The core of our activities is, after all, our will striving for something. This is the point of departure of all that we do. St Benedict does not judge the moral dimension of desiring or wanting. They are a dynamic force, open to being used and managed. We may wish for both that which is good and for that which is evil. St Benedict thus talks about good and evil desires. It is necessary to give direction to our internal dynamic of emotions – so fragile and so susceptible to accepting any cargo of values. Not infrequently, emotions are the sphere and the expression of our hurt. As we have said earlier, pain eagerly makes use of them to indicate its presence. And the reverse is true – emotions equally willingly "feed" on our hurt, simply wanting to demonstrate their presence. The quality of life with someone is the quality of managing and using emotions – so that they should help us to become closer to each other rather than more distant. It has been said that the quality of life of a community (including the Benedictines) is proven not by the absence of conflicts, but by the ability to resolve them. We need no reminding about the key role played by emotions in such situations. They can push the whole matter to one side or another. Again, one can and should see here traces of the Paschal way: the pain and difficulty which purify. The rain, the storm, allow us to appreciate better the beauty of a fine morning. Similarly,

---

13 Cf. L. Natali, *Desiderio e/o volontà: un cammino dialettico perto? 'Desiderare'/ 'Desiderium' – 'Velle'/'Voluntas': una rilettura semantica e simbolica della Regula Benedictini*, Excerptum ex Dissertatione ad Doctoratum Sacrae Theologiae assequendum in Pontifico Athenaeo S. Anselmi, Roma 2003.

passing through the meanders of emotions allows us to reach the hidden possibilities and goodness in ourselves, and in other people. The treacherous spaces of emotions can be entryways to grace. They help to activate our potential, making it possible to discover new spaces of our freedom and brotherly love. It is necessary to pass through the drama of Good Friday in order to experience the full joy of the morning of the Resurrection. And while emotions are eager to combine with the darkest aspects of human nature, it is also necesssary to quote a sentence from St Paul's letter to the Romans: *That as sin hath reigned to death; so also grace might reign by justice* (Rom 5,21). Emotions, and the effort linked to them may in this way become a space of prayer and trust. One need only see their true, the widest possible, context.

In his *Rule*, St Benedict presents a situation which must have been familiar to him from experience. It is both unequivocal and moving in equal measure:

> *And if a brother be punished in any way by the Abbot or by any of his Superiors for even a slight reason or if he perceive that the temper of any of his Superiors is but slightly ruffled or excited against him in the least, let him without delay cast himself down on the ground at his feet making satisfaction, until the agitation is quieted by a blessing.* (RulBen 71, 5–7).

Emotions, turbulence, are something normal even in the most ordinary relationships. What is important is the ability to stand outside them, or at least to rise above them for a moment, so as to see the other person, and even perhaps the hurt we might cause by our emotions. In the situation described above, emotions and the tension linked to them finally become the reason for giving, and receiving, a blessing. It happens sometimes – unfortunately, with increasing frequency – that the unrestrained emotions of a subordinate terrorise a superior. What is most important is that, regardless of what went on before, someone should decide to enter the path to conciliation. Otherwise, as we know, emotions undergo escalation. This is hardly surprising, since they are the fruit of our traumas, complexes or blockages. Also here, what is needed very much are patience, sensitivity, goodwill and mercy, in order to reshape emotions into a constructive motion which ultimately leads to harmony and to that which is positive.

Although often we do not know why we explode, there always is a cause. Presenting the "instruments of good works", St Benedict s foresees a number of possible emotional "explosions". He thus recommends in his *Rule* that monks should not give way to anger (4,22), do nothing motivated by envy (4,66), that they should dislike quarrels (4,67) – and if one does take place, they should make up before sunset (4,72).

Using a classical Biblical image, our struggle with emotions may be compared to the crossing of the Red Sea by the Israelites. The necessity of breaking away from that in which we are grounded, and the fear of going into the unknown that accompanies this, turn out – whether we want it or not – to be the only path to victorious crossing through the waves of emotion. This finds a telling illustration in Chopin's scherzi, where strong contrast between component parts constitutes the principle of construction and expression. The first part, usually repeated later to close the form, is full of turbulent, almost "seething" emotions. They flow as a wide stream, gather, break up. It is difficult to say with certainty what it is that they express: passion, violence, rebellion, despair? Of course, everything is under control, conducted according to consciously adopted principles. However, the power of the emotions expressed by Chopin in these works is quite singular.

And just as the expression of these emotions is so intense, so very much awaited and necessary is the contrast created by the "nocturnal" middle part, bringing an image of emotions that have been ordered and tamed. Its character is very special in *Scherzo in B minor* op. 20, which we have mentioned previously. In it, Chopin quotes the carol-lullaby *Lulajże, Jezuniu*.

If we juxtapose its sound and all the meanings carried by its melody with the extraordinary intensity of emotion of the outlying parts (i.e., that "thundering on the piano"), we obtain the classical picture of healing, or rather the transforming of emotions, which we tried to describe. A similar constructional-expressive device is used in the other scherzos. In the second and third ones, the focused concentration of the middle part is emphasised by introducing a narration which brings associations with the chorale.

In the fourth scherzo that healing role belongs to the wide expanse of a nocturne.

It does not matter that after this calming of emotion there is the return of the turbulence of the first part, made even more dense towards the end of the work. After all, that is how things happen in life: there is always more emotion than calm. And yet moments of healing are possible, and the memory of them helps us bear even the worst of emotions, believing that they do not have the last word. And even if they do, it is only to make sure that they disappear for good.

The Details

One of the achievements of the plastic arts which cleared the way for modernity is undoubtedly that of making the detail independent, and at times assigning to it an important rank. Approaching the subject somewhat perversely, this might mean turning the existing order upside down. For expression, however, this was an important step. It allowed the artist to turn attention to things which were usually marginalised, to reveal the hidden essence of objects or situations. The first painter who began to shock by highlighting the detail on a larger scale was Caravaggio. Today, we see in him a precursor of modern framing. His ideas for approaching classical themes disturbed his contemporaries. In the scene of *The Conversion of St Paul*, in the central plane we find … the rear end of a horse. In *Madonna of the Pilgrims*, it is the dirty feet of the pilgrims kneeling in front of Mary that are closest to the viewer. Examples could be multiplied. It is as if the artist was consciously teasing the stereotypical expectations of how these themes should be depicted. His aim is to show new aspects of the scene he presents, and thus he purposely brings to the fore that which seems unimportant, in order to force the viewer to seek new associations, and thus to find new meanings hidden in a given scene. And one has to admit that such an artistic strategy allows one to reach ever-new areas of that which is inexpressible. In a sense, it is here that art and mysticism touch and penetrate each other – reaching (in essence, blindly) towards the Mystery, but with a portent of the concrete. It is important not to trap the meaning of this message in dead formulae, as well as not to say too much. What matters is the awakening of curiosity, an indication of the existence of something deeper or further, an invitation to cross the threshold of sensory stimuli and of that which can be easily controlled by the intellect. In such a context, the role of the detail – well chosen and emphasised – is particularly momentous.

Before we try to show how such expressiveness, achieved through detail, functions in Chopin's music, let us think for a moment about how we listen, what is our reception of music. Much has been written on this issue, and it is still the subject of wide-ranging research. Approaching it synthetically, what is important in listening is our experience, or musical knowledge, sensitivity, perspicacity – but also intelligence. That is because music is created according to certain principles. The more aware of them we are, and the better we know them, the more and better we hear. It should also be acknowledged that at least an elementary knowledge of these principles is a necessary condition of any sensible reception of music.

Here the composer himself, or herself, comes to our aid, whether consciously or not. The composer's work consists in planning a particular discourse, which needs to be sufficiently comprehensible and interesting to make the listener want to follow the composer's idea. In this sense, music is a constant interplay between the composer and the listener, as has clearly been shown by Leonard B. Meyer[14]. The binding principles here result primarily from the psychological and acoustic features of human perception of music[15], and these are, in a sense, rooted in the basic mechanisms of our consciousness and our existence. When we begin to listen to a particular work, we are usually prepared by the composer for accepting the main motif or theme. This is done through an introduction, which does not tell us very much. However, when a theme does appear, the listener has to become thoroughly acquainted with it, and this is achieved through a repetition of the theme, as well as through emphasising its characteristic aspects in a variety of ways. There then appears contrasting material, the familiar motifs undergo minor or major changes, which in turn produce expressive effects. If we bear in mind that this can happen on a number of different levels, simultaneously or successively, music turns out to be a set of many events, a multi-threaded discourse with the composer as its organiser and coordinator. And, as happens in such complex artistic situations, the resulting reception does not necessarily correspond to the artist's intentions. However, if a common platform of understanding compositional actions and the listener's reception is established, it is possible to optimise that complex and delicate event – one might say, encounter – which is listening to music. With the proviso, however, that the essence of possible communication remains elusive and unique.

Let us, however, return to the question of detail, since this is precisely what plays such an important role in the shaping and development of musical discourse. The introduction of any new material, any changes in it, any perceptible differences or similarities – all these are the result of discreet and consistent action of many details. Not surprising then that a masterly interpretation can be recognised at once by the attention to detail, regardless of what this might involve in terms of compositional technique. In order to see what might be involved, let us briefly analyse the beginning of *Mazurka in A minor* op. 17 No. 4. Its texture is transparent. The discourse begins as early as the introductory part of the accompaniment. The slight movement of the melodic line creates a mood of

---

14 L.B. Meyer, *Emotion and meaning in music*, Chicago 1961.
15 Cf. the volume by E. Ansermet, *Les fondaments de la musique dans la conscience humanie et autres écrits*, Paris 1989, which is fundamental in this area.

expectancy and openness – with an admixture, however, of a little melancholy. It is only on top of this that the composer superimposes the main melodic line, in small phrases, as if being added together, or expanding. There is restraint in it, but also some inner imperative. In spite of everything, the development of the melody here takes place precisely through the interplay of detail. The same motif undergoes modifications, and their course directs the line of discourse.

A similar situation can be seen in the texture of *Prelude in E minor* op. 28 No. 4. Although here the melody begins together with the accompaniment, its development takes place on the plane of minor changes within basically repeating motifs. In order to hear this development, one needs concentration and great sensitivity, but perceiving it produces a powerful feeling of peace and harmony with an admixture of inner dynamic. This music may seem static, but it unmistakably pulsates with an inner life of its own. (**Prelude in E minor* op. 28 No. 4)

In both these works we can see how detail, and the small changes in it, determine not only the whole of the mood of the composition, but discreetly and irrevocably constitute the musical discourse. Our hearing, our memory, are in this way drawn into a subtle game. Deviations, their perception, their size, become the space in which the encounter between the composer and the listener takes place, but they are also the carriers of expression. Each note is important because, being a result of a change, it may be a carrier of an important component of expression. Sometimes it hides under the seemingly motionless line of the melody, passing into the layer of harmony and its vibrations and displacements, hardly perceptible in the tectonics of the chords. This makes the challenge to the listener's sensitivity all the greater, but is also a greater risk for the composer. However, when successful, the effect is particularly appealing. It is like receiving an invitation to journey somewhere into the interior.

It is also possible to develop a number of levels with intense expression in one work. In such cases, the richness of details, and their mutual relationships, seem limitless. The narration is a panoramic, multicoloured movement. The changes are then perceived in another dimension. They have to be more distinct, taking in many details, whole constellations of them. But also here, nothing will make sense unless it takes into account our capability to perceive. Both large changes and the most subtle ones are limited by the threshold of our musical and perceptual sensitivity. In every case, however, the sound transmission may become for us a momentous study of sensitivity and consistency (or faithfulness). This is because of the necessity to pay attention to the smallest detail, and faithfulness to it – as a recognition of the subtlety of the form of organisation and order.

In monastic life, which in a sense is monotonous and rhythmical because of its regularity, one naturally develops a subtle sensitivity and creativity corresponding to the inner openness needed to live in a world which is highly regulated externally. In such a situation, it is the play of details and their interaction that make sensitivity possible. This happens above all at the level of communication. It is essential to maintain a balance between that which is external and internal, between that which is individual and communal. Transparency and clarity in this area are the necessary conditions for developing true interaction between people, which is particularly important in a life that is shared with others. This is the most desirable basis for Benedictine obedience. Sensitivity and trust need to be helped, they have to be nurtured, which in practice means – again! – attention to detail and, at a further stage, providing a space of goodwill and brotherly love. It manifests itself in the most ordinary gestures, smiles and expressions which seem imperceptible. However, it is they which create an atmosphere of closeness, understanding, and purposeful shared activity. The more restricted a group or a community of a limited number of persons (which in a monastic reality is quite normal), the greater the resonance of these minor gestures, even though originally they function on the microscale of personal relationships. Undoubtedly this places on one an obligation to be as alert, sensible and responsible as possible. The matter of human relationships is particularly delicate; one thus has to foresee potentially sensitive points or subjects, and avoid touching on them where possible. What is at stake is people's reactions, but also the transmission of information which others may interpret in a manner totally different from that intended by the sender.

These remarks apply both to the Benedictine reality, and to Chopin's music. In the centre of attention of both is the human being and human affairs, which most often and most basically means human relationships. Attention to detail and its message is usually the subject of penetrating observation by outsiders. This concerns both listening to music and contacts between people and monks. The pain lies in the fact that details so easily slip out of our control, and yet they are sometimes the first and the most convincing signal that informs others about us. They are thus a chance, easily lost, of establishing contact with someone else which can only mean that they are extremely important, regardless from which side we view them. An area where details are of particular importance is care for the sick and for the weakest but also, by analogy, another area are compositions with a structure that is fragile, whether by design or lack of explicitness. Where there is no daring, no great, general causes – or where there is no wider perspective of a clearly delineated form – everything happens, as we have already mentioned, through detail. The impossibility of encompassing the totality, the absence of a key to understanding the full set of details, "condemns" us to humble, individual sensitivity to them, which undoubtedly may be a great difficulty. And that also underlines again the importance of details. There are good grounds for saying that "the devil is in the details". Neglecting them usually destroys the larger and more complex forms put together with great effort. In our practical life, this may mean unnecessary emotions, most often anger, and long-term frustrations. Also from this perspective, a detail may, paradoxically, become a space where relationships are shaped, expressing goodwill and love. How we approach it may turn out to be a means of, or a factor in, improving or worsening our relationships. In this way we reach the amazing dependence of that which is inexpressible (i.e., the quality of relationships) on minor, seemingly meaningless scraps of matter. In a sense this brushes against mysticism, which often arises in the crevices of the incomprehensible, between opposite poles that are difficult to reconcile. Going beyond what can be done, crossing the limits that point us towards transcendence, also opens the gates to mysticism, a space which is open to contemplation but which potentially also opens up ourselves (if we take up its challenge).

It gives one pause, how much the text of the *Rule*, like the text of the Bible, can be saturated with details. They are always intriguing, ultimately turning out to be carriers of some message. In the text in which they are grounded, details turn out to be the points which draw attention, sometimes strained by the constant attempts to encompass the whole and operate on a general level. A detail, often startling and striking in its distinctiveness, evokes the question *why?* and makes one penetrate deeper. In this way we begin to pause in our reading, and, through the crevice opened up by that detail, we seem to penetrate deep into the text, beginning its exploration. Many such images are present even in the psalms, the basic texts of prayers at a Benedictine monastery. Here are a few examples taken from a number of consecutive psalms:

> *What will he [God] do to you, and what more besides, you deceitful tongue?*
> *He will punish you with a warrior's sharp arrows,*
> *with burning coals of the broom bush.* (Ps 120[11 9],3–4).
> *We have escaped like a bird from the fowler's snare;*
> *the snare has been broken, and we have escaped.* (Ps 124[123],7).
> *Ploughmen have ploughed my back and made their furrows long.* (Ps 129[128],3).

The small, distinctive associations shown here have the character of impressions. The concreteness of the images with which they operate makes it easier for them to emerge easily from the background of a content which is basically general. Yet it is concrete objects with which we most often have to deal. It is no surprise that ordinary everyday reality wants to penetrate the discourse of the text in this particular way. Not just that, but through it we have effective access to the past. Concrete objects are the messengers between our present and that past. They allow us access to the Proustian "lost time". More often than not, this brings pain, touching some wound, but it is always a chance to return to something important and close. This is another mystical space which combines contradictions, matters "irretrievably lost", and the open present. The yearning for an impossible synthesis is, after all, an important dimension of mysticism. It is at the same time a yearning for an encounter, for uniting irreconcilables. Details are the privileged places of meetings, crossings, dialogue, where paths from different levels and different areas of reality can come together. For them, details become moments of integration, a space of dialogue. They allow a meeting between everyday life and contemplation, fleetingness and eternity. They thus cannot be absent from the conscious experience within the framework of Benedictine life, but also within any human existence. They make our lives real and concrete, they define their practical course, at the same time becoming a place that is open to an encounter with Transcendence – with God. That is the way to understand the very precise instructions from the fourth chapter of the *Rule: The Instruments of Good Works*: "To chastise the body. Not to seek after pleasures. (…) Not to give way to anger. Not to foster a desire for revenge. Not to entertain deceit in the heart." (RulBen 4,11 –12.22–24). This is a description of concrete situations or attitudes, like a practical summary of ethical divagations – the necessity of taking an unequivocal stance, without the possibility of evasion or compromise. In the temporal dimension these are points – details, moments sometimes palpably present, experienced and remembered. They resemble, by their eloquence and the powerful nature of the shot, contemporary films, both psychological ones and… thrillers, which, along the same lines as Caravaggio, delight in shots that are sharp, abbreviated, sometimes shocking, sometimes purposefully intensified, exaggerated or clipped, sometimes aggressive. Telediscs or videoclips are moving in that direction, using images which accompany powerful rhythmic music. It is interesting to see how important details are here, how quickly shots with their various shapes follow each other, and how demanding and rigorous are the ways in which they are presented, framed and changed. Sequences of images seem to be jumping from one "core" of the detail to the next. The aim is to achieve the highest possible power of expression, trying to reach almost the very heart of the viewer. There is an amazing kinship between such treatment of detail and the medieval art of illuminating manuscripts. In both we have a small form with simultaneous and necessary intensification of expression. In both cases there is a similar desirable openness to mysticism, however one might understand it. The line of Caravaggio's shots seems to widen and deepen going equally into the past as into the future. Through detail, we can travel through various areas of human expression and history, through various forms of expression of spirituality. That which is inexpressible hides itself in details. It is a trace of the presence of God. Medieval artists had good reason for placing ornamental detail, finished with great care, on the roofs of cathedrals, even though no human eye could see it. A well-finished detail, pregnant with meaning, can become a messenger between heaven and earth. If we look at our life from that point of view, each day, each moment, is of importance. St Benedict describes this very suggestively, saying: "Let a man consider that (…) the eye of God beholdeth his works everywhere, and that the angels report them to Him every hour." (RulBen 7,20–21). Whether we like it or not, our life is a spectacle in which every detail counts. Everything may turn out to be important, everything may significantly influence how we and our relationships are perceived.

Another form of concern about detail is demonstrated by the following words in the *Rule*, relating to the cellarer, or the monk responsible for the material goods in the monastery:

> *Let him regard all the vessels of the monastery and all its substance, as if they were sacred vessels of the altar. Let him neglect nothing ...* (RulBen 31, 11–13).

We can see how, in concern over detail, we have an unexpected meeting between two seemingly distant realities – that of the liturgy, and that of everyday. Detail as a carrier of God's affairs plays a very important part in the *Rule*, but also in the Benedictine tradition as a whole. The architecture of Benedictine monasteries, always finished off and cared for in the minutest detail, taking on the responsibility for the purposeful life enclosed within it, testifies to this link powerfully and constantly. Detail can thus be an expression of concern for the human being in this form, as well as being a place of practical and concrete encounter with beauty in the context of everyday reality. It is thanks to this that we can, to some extent, travel through the landscapes of the mysticism of life filled with the supernatural light of God's presence.

At this point we are ready to sum up these reflections with a comprehensive example from Chopin's music. It gathers in itself the use of detail characteristic of many of Chopin's works. This is *Grande Valse brillante in E-flat major* op. 18, perhaps the most representative and classical of all Chopin waltzes. It is music woven from sparkling details. The formal framework on the macroscale seems to be a pretext for subtle narration taking place at the level of details and their mutual interaction. There we find much natural and touching concern, present seemingly without effort but very sensitive and full of imagination. The narration and the form of the waltz, by the very nature of their practical aim, have a standard character, since this music is meant to be danced (even if, as in the case of Chopin's composition, it is stylised). It is the details that make the narration of the waltz dynamic. One might say that they gather into themselves all that for which the waltz is a pretext – the desire and the opportunity of closeness, the looks, the gestures, the hints, the enchantment, the flirting. Their multi-shaped, multi-coloured nature is still only a weak reflection of human inventiveness. Here ease combines with necessity, pleasure with sensitivity. The scintillation of the details, subtle though it is, is so enchanting as to make time seem suspended. If we have the impression of it flowing, it is only through the fluctuation of changes in the details. Everything here has a light but festive character, elegant and open; we are participating in some inevitable festival, which encompasses everything with a smile. A festival, or holiday-making, is nothing but joyful concern for relationships. The waltz demonstrates their greatest beauty, the ultimate horizon of what can take place between people. Should not our life have something of a waltz about it? Day-to-day reality lit up by detail, lived creatively and with enthusiasm – perhaps that is the only condition of experiencing the taste of life to the full, and not only in a Benedictine monastery. Chopin's waltzes testify to the composer being only too familiar with that taste, so it is hardly surprising that the illness which was taking over his life must have been all the more painful. The expression of pain, of yearning, gradually deformed the joyful directness of the details which, as we recall, form the essence of waltz. Everything in it, however, is permeated with a delicate yet distinct aura of mysticism – opening up to another, meeting them, forming a bond. Is it not, then, also a space for contemplating the creativity and the presence of God Himself, unpretentiously hidden in the sounds of a waltz? (*Grande Valse brillante in E-flat major* op. 18)

The Melody – A Treatise on Embodied Grace

The thesis contained in the title might seem somewhat exaggerated. However, if we wish to develop fully the analogy between Chopin's music and the meanings contained in St Benedict's *Rule*, such theological consequences should not come as a surprise. And there should be nothing strange about the need to pay special attention to Chopin's melodies – with the proviso that their extraordinariness (or, why not say it, their genius) by its very nature escapes any attempt at analysis. However, it is still worth trying since – in comparison with the achievements of other excellent melodists, such as Bach, Mozart, Schumann or Brahms – the phenomenon of Chopinian melody is one of a kind. Outstanding melodies may have a very "designed" and moderate character (Bach, Brahms). We then find in their beginnings a clearly delineated, almost a cosmic rhythm, which then carries and leads the given melody. All that is left for the listener to do is to surrender to such a melody, which is facilitated by its well-organised structure. There are also melodies which are simply heavenly – natural and spellbinding in their unearthly charm, appearing from no-one-knows-where (Mozart, Schubert). Others, akin to them, have the character of a fairy tale (Schumann, Brahms). We feel that we already know them from somewhere, and they affect the imagination in a singular way. Chopin's melodies have some features from each of these groups, and this, paradoxically, makes them both unique and natural. This is also a mysterious feature of melodies with the mark of genius: our greatest admiration comes from their simplicity that is refined but not unnatural. Melodies of these musicians are characterised by what might be called a degree of perfection. In their way, they are extreme in their expression, in a positive sense of the word. Chopin's melodics is never extreme. Its genius is more to do with moderation. While creating melodies that are orderly but with something heavenly or fairytale about them, Chopin succeeded in maintaining restraint, not associating himself with any particular, characteristic expression which would not be "his kind". This restraint seems to correspond to the Benedictine principle of moderation. Preserving moderation, in combination with an awareness of the available possiblities, is something both deeply human and close to all of us. Such are, as we have said, both Chopin's music and the instructions of St Benedict's *Rule*, while the human dimension we have just mentioned has in it a nobility and loftiness. It does not embarrass or humiliate, but, rather, points to that which is most splendid and at the same time most delicate in humankind. In this way we can see how earthly matters unite with heavenly ones. Not strange then that in Chopin's melodies there must be as much loftiness as yearning, as much power as fragility. And yet in our life, in its most aware, greatest moments, these spheres – the human and transcendent realities – penetrate each other. Hence the kinship that is of so much interest to us, between Chopin's music and the meanings of St Benedict's *Rule*. As we can see, both realities are equally suspended "between heaven and earth".

Some of Chopin's phrases, in spite of their naturalness and moderation, appear as if from nowhere – as if, in an almost obvious way, they were inspired by some unearthly reality. And they appear like a breath, like the wind: *The wind bloweth where it listeth, and thou hearest the sound thereof, but canst not tell whence it cometh, and whither it goeth* (John 3,8) – and in this breeze there is as much lightness as sensuality, as much poignancy as discretion. This is the nature of *Prelude in C-sharp minor* op. 28 No.10, which literally lasts only one moment. (**Prelude in C-sharp minor* op. 28 No. 10). Is there a melody there, or is it its breath wafting on the breeze? A breath bound into actual sounds by a spell, or perhaps sounds set free by the touch of a non-material breath? This kind of expression is typical of impressionistic music. The melody points to a reality beyond it. However, for this to be possible there must be some strong inspiration, unobtrusive yet sufficiently concrete to be ready to adopt a specific musical shape. An inspiration – or an idea, a concept – which seeks and finds the right material "shape" (*Gestalt*) is a motif present in the theology of Hans Urs von Balthasar[16]. It perceives the figure of Christ precisely in terms of a "shape", a perfect materialisation (speaking theologically, an "embodiment", a "form") of the Idea (the "Word"). It is the synthesis we have talked about earlier in its pure form – a new quality consisting in the encounter between that which is physical and bodily and that which is spiritual and Divine. The touch of the Spirit, in order to reveal itself, needs, almost demands, a concrete bodily reality. We would like Chopin's melody to serve as an analogy of just such an event – just as St Benedict's *Rule* wants to bring that event closer to the practical, everyday life.

Let us then take a closer look at melody and its course. Why, how does it move us, what makes it beautiful and enchanting? Why do we like it? There are no exhaustive answers to these questions, but we need to ask them to make our deliberations range over the widest possible horizon. At the same time we are trying to describe, as far as this is possible, how melody "works". It appeals to us by its lightness, at the same time giving us the feeling of being something important in itself, of being one of a kind, gifted with an exceptional shape, knowledge of which gives us joy

---

16   Cf. footnote 4.

and satisfaction. Delicacy and mystery are combined with tangibility – just as active grace must encounter the resistance and heaviness (*pesanteur*, to use Simone Weil's term[17]) of matter. The two realities seem to need each other; they serve each other. The most intriguing, and most significant in the context of these reflections, is their point of contact – a touch, a movement, mysterious, graceful, irrevocable and effective, subtle yet strong, delicate yet concrete. This is exactly what happens in so many of Chopin's compositions. Often a given melody takes full possession of us from the beginning, immediately, without asking and without scruples. This is what takes place in such works as *Waltz in A-flat major* op. 69 No. 1:

Mazurka in A minor op. 67 No. 4:

or *Nocturne in F minor* op. 55 No. 1:

Perhaps this is simply a return to some state that is the original state for us, some misplaced but natural reminiscence of a lost – paradise? Childhood? To be honest, we are always close to the radiant influence of grace, which constantly and

---

17   Cf. S. Weil, *La pesanteur et la grâce*, Paris (1947[1]) 1991.

humbly invites us with the words: *Come, follow me!*, which we cannot resist. Each moment when something speaks to us and, as a result, we decide on a change, is extremely powerful. This is a familiar, classic situation in the Gospels: the moments of being called, of meeting Jesus, meeting His look. It takes so little, yet everything is different. Those who undergo this encounter are captured, carried off – a new chapter begins in their life. This situation is described very vividly in Preface for Christmas I, as these holy days are a time particularly susceptible to enchantment: "In the wonder of the incarnation your eternal Word has brought to the eyes of faith a new and radiant vision of Your glory. In Him we see our God made visible and so are caught up in love of the God we cannot see." Christmas is a remembrance of a situation which we are trying to describe, in which God, being invisible, revealed himself to us in a human body. Moving from that which is invisible to the visible – the revelation of the Invisible – is one of the most mysterious and intriguing aspects of the workings of grace. As we try to describe it here, the situation works both ways: man tries to reach the inexpressible through that which can be seen, and that which cannot be seen (the Divine) tries to show itself in various ways. The two situations are joined by the moment of rapture, based, often starting imperceptibly, in that which is most natural. That moment is an opening and the most beautiful fruit of sensitivity. It shows that, in their essence, things physical and sensual, somewhere at their deepest, are rooted in that which is supranatural. Very many of Chopin's melodies seem to refer to somewhere higher and further, beyond their sound itself, in an obvious and natural way. They may be fleeting, but this combines in the strangest way with a very concrete melodic shape, the uniqueness and refinement of the formulae used with the feeling of their moving closeness. This happens, for example, in *Fantasie-impromptu in C-sharp minor* op. 66, a work which has in it some exaltation, quite unlike Chopin, but the main motif of which carries a great and captivating power, even though in itself it gives the impression of being delicate and flexible. (**Fantasie-impromptu in C-sharp minor* op. 66)

A powerful sign of this "presence of grace" is the extraordinary richness – almost overabundance, or limitless creativity, of Chopin's melodies. Few composers could lay claim to this. Listening to new ideas or musical motifs which keep pouring out we have the impression of taking part in some imaginative game being tirelessly played with us – but by whom? By the composer – or perhaps by the One in whose name, as we might have grounds to believe, he is acting? It is interesting to note that the greatest melodists (Mozart and Chopin) we have talked about here were deeply aware that they were only the depositaries of talent – the music which they were to pass on.

Examining the phenomenon of melody at a deeper level we come across a paradox. Even though we are trailing that which is fleeting and unearthly, rules are still essential. In order to create a melody we have to, consciously or not, follow certain principles. Melody owes its beauty and captivating grace to the freedom achieved by obeying these rules. They are usually described as the "craft". As is the case with every master, it is only by acquiring the arcana that one can become creative, making it possible to give beauty a permanent and perceptible shape. It is necessary to be ruthless here: even in difficult or extreme situations, rules cannot be bypassed. They serve that greater something which arises on their foundations, but beyond or even in spite of them. The melody which captivates us always seems to bypass the rules, but we can try and "target" it when we know these rules. The freedom, originality and communicativeness of a given melody would not be possible unless it fits into some rules – constructional, rhythmic, harmonic, or the principles of building up tension. The analogy with Benedictine life (i.e., also life according to the *Rule*) comes to mind naturally. We may touch the mystery of grace becoming real, embodied, precisely here, in the game between human freedom and the principles – or laws – of nature which are given to humankind in one way or another. The greater the number of limitations, the greater the opportunity for revealing the power and freedom of action of grace in man. That which is the most brilliant, and at the same time the most captivating, manifests itself using minimal means. Simplicity and sophistication are combined directly. This is what happens, for example, in the Gregorian melody of the preface – it consists of only four notes, and yet one can listen to it constantly without becoming bored. A similar situation arises with the choral Mass melody of *Pater noster*. In both cases, a minimum of material expresses a maximum of content.

Of course, it is impossible to live at such a high volume of expression all the time. However, the awareness that it exists, and choosing it as one's goal, is an essential component of human dignity and greatness. Constant longing for beauty and the striving towards it is inextricably linked to the deepest and truest aspirations of our life. It is not only an invitation, but the ultimate limit of our aspirations. We can only realise them effectively if we follow specific rules, like a painter painting an icon. The effort of limitedness and adaptation turns out to be an essential condition of encountering and expressing beauty. St Benedict sees that the obstacles caused by the limits imposed by the *Rule* are there to give us a space of inner freedom. It is for this reason that even the beginning of the *Rule* contains words full of hope and encouragement:

> ...*if, to correct vices or to preserve charity, sound reason dictateth anything that turneth out somewhat stringent, do not at once fly in dismay from the way of salvation,*

> *the beginning of which cannot but be narrow (Matt. 7:14). But as we advance in the religious life and faith, we shall run the way of God's commandments with expanded hearts and unspeakable sweetness of love;* (RulBen Prologue 50–53)

Reaching the fullness of spiritual matters carries a cost. It is reached through difficulties experienced largely because of our human circumstances and limitations. Undertaking a life that leads in that direction is like walking a tightrope. The direction seems clear, but uncertainty and risk hover over every step of the way. Probably this experience is close to any committed artistic activity, as well as undertaking any ambitious project. The proper space for such experiences in a Benedictine monastery is the liturgy. The objective space of words and gestures is shaped by the sum of personal commitments. The resultant of the sensitivities of all the participants of the liturgical action brings the final shape, experienced externally. Both such commitment to liturgy and the response to it must be accompanied by risk. However, a courageous undertaking of it may in effect bring a satisfaction that would have been unimaginable previously – an experience of something more than could be achieved by oneself. The line of tension runs thus not just between the inexpressible and the expressible, but also between the individual and the community. This is nothing other than the struggle to keep the balance or, speaking in Benedictine terms, a concern for maintaining moderation. Using descriptions from the fragment of the *Rule* quoted above, it is a path that leads from efforts, even from a hardened heart, to a heart expanded with love: a prospect desired by everyone who cares about their life and development.

This important moment is also described by St Benedict in the seventh chapter of the *Rule*, showing from another aspect the process of moving from difficulty and effort to the ease which is brought by love. It is also a description of the situation in which a monk finds himself after traversing all the twelve degrees of humility:

> *Having, therefore, ascended all these degrees of humility, the monk will presently arrive at that love of God, which being perfect, casteth out fear (1 Jn 4:18). In virtue of this love all things which at first he observed not without fear, he will now begin to keep without any effort, and as it were, naturally by force of habit, no longer from the fear of hell, but from the love of Christ, from the very habit of good and the pleasure in virtue. May the Lord be pleased to manifest all this by His Holy Spirit in His laborer now cleansed from vice and sin.* (RulBen 7, 84–87).

Let us examine that mechanism of the transformation of effort and difficulties into the experience of ease which comes as a result of the working of grace. This is a concrete example of palpable and truly tangible results of its action – difficult to express, being highly individualised, but undoubtedly possible and probably described by St Benedict on the basis of his own experience.

At this point we might – and should – return to the music of Chopin, gathering together the above thoughts in an analysis of a particular composition. This is *Etude in E-flat major* op. 10 No. 11, transparent in its form, although very sophisticated in terms of the technical demands it makes on the performer. The ordinary effect of leading a simple melodic line is to be achieved by overcoming the meanders of widely spaced chords, which in addition have to be played arpeggio. The difficulty, the almost internal contradiction of this musical challenge, consists in achieving simplicity of musical expressiveness by using extremely complex means of expression. In practice, this means that one has to play lightly at least six notes quite distant from each other, drawing the line of the melody from combined notes of the highest voice which, by virtue of its position and the manner of playing, is the weakest. It is as if that which is the most beautiful and most moving hid itself in the most fragile form, and wanted to reveal itself from just such a paradoxical hiding place. Regardless of the effort necessary to achieve the right artistic effect when playing this etude, one should also mention the perhaps less obvious effort of listening to it: in both cases the main line of the melody has to be, in a sense, "abstracted" from the rich texture of the chords which mark the flow of the composition as a whole. This should be an encounter between the endeavour (effort) by the performer and the attention of the listener. The creation and transmission of the expressiveness of this composition thus depends on the encounter between two efforts, as well as two sensitivities: one might say, a double fragility which seems to be the destined fate of this composition. But if it is undertaken and used with humility, the effect achieved cannot be expressed in just its natural categories. If one is aware of this effort, at least on the performer's side, the effect of amazement and delight is all the greater. Let this, however, be only an analogy (or perhaps so much as an analogy) of our greatest and most risky actions, which we carry out every day. If we succeed in this, both Chopin's music and the instructions of St Benedict's *Rule* will turn out to be equally helpful. (**Etude in E-flat major* op.10 No. 11)

Let us try to sum up the above reflections with an attempt to answer the question: in what does a melody really consist? How does it allow us to understand – or perhaps experience - the embodiment of grace? A melody is the shape given to a reality lacking shape. It is an acoustic attempt to capture the inexpressible, to arrange some kind of a whole out of disordered fragments. The very effort of capturing, of recording the inexpressible is already an attempt to be faithful to the inexpressible Mystery, a declaration of being on the side of the embodied grace. Its possibility and its presence make us seek an opportunity of preserving at least a trace of it. Who knows, perhaps music is the best means of achieving this – being itself fleeting, could it, modestly and discreetly, lend its form to the inexpressible? This is not easy, since an encounter with the Mystery is, above all, our own, sometimes very private, experience. The action of grace is directed towards an individual, and is realised in a particular situation. How can this be captured, transmitted, made permanent? We have mentioned that the fleetingness and fragility of music give it that right. But is it enough? It is also necessary to have the right predisposition and readiness both of the artist and the recipient, so that a harmonious shape can arise out of the unordered fragments, like the magnetic field which orders the pieces of metal. A melody is thus, in a sense, the medium which links us to transcendence. But it is also an expression of synthesis, its fruit and its path. As we can see, it combines many threads of meaning, hence its importance. When it has the right shape it enchants, when it does not achieve it, it is very distasteful.

Very often we are not happy with our own life – its events, contacts with others. We experience many conflicts, consciously or unconsciously not making contact with those with whom we have to live or act together. The reason for this state of affairs is most often our lack of detachment and perspective. We are too closely entangled in the practical affairs of our life, and we cannot see the true reason for the conflict or difficulty. Quite frequently it comes from outside and, in order to become aware of it, we need to detach ourselves from that which usually surrounds us. That, however, carries a cost. It also carries a risk, since it means entering the unknown. Yet detachment, breaking away from our ordinary surroundings, is a portal not only to reflection, but to contemplation. Melody helps us achieve that distance. Alluring in its beauty, melody makes us follow it in order to show us, from its own perspective, far removed from mundane matters, all that is incomprehensible and painful in our everyday reality. This is how, as we have mentioned before, it appears in many of Chopin's works – often from the very beginning, immediately and without a "by your leave" taking possession of our attention and, sometimes, even all of ourselves. In this way we become not only "pulled away from the earth", but we may also try to get closer to that which is Divine. The more captivating, the more unearthly a melody – the more detachment from mundane matters it gives us and helps us to keep. This helps us to view reality more as a whole, to comprehend more, and become more patient and understanding. Life without detachment is possible only in a space of trust – in the belief that someone else sees more, and more widely. In both cases we are dealing with the attitude of an "expanded heart" mentioned earlier which, in the spiritual tradition is, in a classical manner, contrasted with a "hardened heart". Perhaps, in truth, this is the only necessary condition for composing a truly beautiful melody, and its proper effect on the listener?

Taking into account the role of the personal context of listening to and experiencing a melody, perhaps it would be best to refrain from presenting a specific example. Each of us can be affected by a different melody. It seems, however, that there are melodies whose power of expression touches everyone. The more paradoxical their structure, the more they seem to be a manifestation of grace. That is the character of the line of the melody in *Prelude in E-flat major* op. 28 No. 19 – almost impossible to play, suspended on chords of expanded, shimmering arabesques. One needs a lot of work and humility to present it clearly, to bring out of the quivering thicket of sounds its delicately but consistently marked flow. What enchants and captivates is the extraordinary simplicity and subtlety of this melody – like a simple song, perhaps being hummed by an angel – emerging so ordinarily but surprisingly from the dense texture of the whole prelude. This music, so very fleeting, lasting only a brief moment, is a most beautiful metaphor of grace in action, breaking through the complex layers of various circumstances and expressions, in order to reign throughout it all, and above it all, by its inexpressible simplicity and nobility. (**Prelude in E-flat major* op. 28 No. 19)

How to End?

Reaching the end of our deliberations, it would perhaps be fitting to devote some attention to the question of endings themselves. The fact that everything comes to an end is not something we ever doubt. However, we know less about how and when to end. Yet this is in many ways an existential subject, although very much neglected. Difficult as it is to make a start, coming to an end can be even harder. Our habits and emotions have great influence in this area. The knowledge that something has been started should evoke an attitude of responsibility. External circumstances are most frequently the problem, but so are our limitations. We are quite often aware how fragile our existence is, and how everything conspires against not only us, but also all our undertakings. Emil Cioran described it in a manner that is both vivid and very true: "Every being emerges from no one knows where, gives out its little cry and disappears without trace".[18] The question about the meaning and permanence of human actions cannot but be linked to the question of the transcendental dimension of our life. Regardless of the answer we give, we experience only too painfully how much we are "on a journey", subject to the flow of time and given little influence on what we do. From an eschatological perspective we might say that the only thing that is certain is death, and that sounds to us pompous at best. In practice, however, contemporary culture and civilisation do everything to move that truth as far as possible, in fact not to see it at all. A clear awareness of the fragility of our existential condition is essential to ensure that all our actions are not only meaningful, but have at least a modicum of a chance of success.

St Benedict is unequivocal here. He recommends that monks should always have their forthcoming death before their eyes (RulBen 4,47). It is one of the instruments of good works, supplemented by guidelines relating to the final, twelfth degree of humility, to feel at every moment guilt for one's sins and consider that one is about to face the dreadful Judgment (ibid. 7, 80–81). One may interpret this as catastrophism or obsession, but also as an expression of responsibility, and thus of high awareness and love of life. It is a tremendous matter not only to fulfil one's tasks responsibly, but also to depart at the right time and in the right manner. The completion of any mission also depends on a reasonably precise definition of its extent, and an awareness of its limits and ending. This concerns

---

18 E. Cioran, *Cahiers 1957–1972*, Paris 1997, p. 456 (author's translation).

also – or perhaps above all – such a special mission as life. We all wish for ourselves the largest number of years of living, but it is a great art to prepare properly for departing and, when the time comes, for reaching the end of one's life. That also was a matter of concern for St Benedict, expressed in the instructions in his *Rule*. In such a perspective, the end may seem harder than the beginning. It requires a preceding continuation, a consistency associated with it, and particular sensitivity and humility. We learn much about this by being with those who are departing, often people who are close to us. Benedictine tradition demands that the abbot takes particular care of the sick (RulBen 36,1). Not surprisingly, he is usually the closest person to the dying, not only to support but, often, also to bear witness. Death reflects life. We prepare for its ending – for every ending – from the beginning.

We should thus be able to ask ourselves questions about our own death. Not only whether we are ready for it, but whether we at least think about it. A good preparation for such a question is our manner – or style – of ending what we started. What is needed here as well is a great deal of asceticism: the ability to leave behind something that we have become used to, which gave us pleasure. Such is the inevitable result of submitting to the flow of time.

It would not be an exaggeration to say that Chopin's music is, in a sense, permeated with death – and we are not talking at all about the yearning, regret or pain which we discussed previously. The physical and psychological experiences which befall a creative artist are not without influence on his creation, and we do know that Chopin fought for a long time an illness which finally killed him prematurely at the age of only thirty-nine. We may wonder whether he accomplished the work of his life; what he would have created had he lived longer. We are left with what he did write at that, and not another, time of his life, fighting his illness and witnessing those, and not any other, political events. At the same time, his music, regardless of that context, has in it much "fulfilment", or even perfection. The poet, C.K. Norwid, claimed "Piętnem globu tego – niedostatek:/Dopełnienie?... go boli!...On – rozpoczynać woli " (*Fortepian Szopena*) "The wretched birthmark of this world is Lack./Him? ... Perfection irks - Prefers - to undo Perfection's works/... Arrests the germination of Art's Act... (*Chopin's Grand Piano*)[19]. It was Chopin's music which he pointed to as a counterbalance. Because, as we know, it

---

19   C.K. Norwid, *Pisma wszystkie*, vol. 2, ed. J.W. Gomulicki, Warszawa 1971, p.145. Translation: http://www.babelmatrix.org/works/pl/Norwid_Cyprian_Kamil/

is not only the beginning which is important in it, but the end – perhaps even more important, not only formally but also existentially.

In many works we can hear not only a lack of acceptance of the necessity of death, but in fact a note of rebellion. Sometimes such a message provides the carrying power of particular music, almost a measure of its greatness. In the most classical way this happens, for example, in the music of Beethoven – and also, in its way, in that of Wagner. Truly, every clearly shaped composition takes its ending very seriously. Leaving aside the question of whether it is an acceptance of the inevitability of the end, or opposition to it, we have to note the special celebration of the ending. Usually it is prepared for by a larger or smaller cadence, or takes on the shape of codas of similar dimensions. Quite often one has the impression that the composer does not want to part with the music being created, or perhaps with the listener as well. As if wanting to look back, full of delight and emotion, at the whole of the presented music, or hurriedly to introduce yet another idea. In a sense, this is a struggle against the necessity, common to all composers, of death in the music, the inevitability of the final dying out of the sounds. Dramatic examples of such conclusions can be found in the endings of *Polonaise in A-flat major* op. 53:

or *Scherzo in B flat minor* op. 31:

They complement very well the turbulent expression of the totality of these compositions. One might say that their shape corresponds to the listener's expectations. Sometimes, however, in similar cases, the composer exaggerates, and the work gives the impression as if, in spite of everything, it still wants to exist, be listened to, influence the listener. It demands this in an insistent, ridiculous manner – as if unable to come to an end, or, rather, endlessly coming to an end. However, there are many compositions which are very humble and modest in their endings, as if they simply accept that everything, including their own sound, must finally cease. In this respect, particularly moving are those works which are characterised by uniform motion. Without breaking out of the discipline of that motion, they end as if they were flying away. Sometimes, at the last moment, like a deeper sigh, there discreetly appears an additional motif, most often an expansion of one of the previous ones. Everything, however, ends as planned and without any problems – perhaps so quickly and ordinarily that the listener might think, "The end already? What a pity!". This is what happens in, for example, *Etudes in F major* op. 10 No. 8:

and op. 25 No. 3:

Everything is and remains fleeting, appears from nowhere and disappears suddenly, no one knows why and where to.

Another example: *Mazurka in C major* op. 24 No. 2. It begins with a small introduction. Then other themes appear, develop, transform into one another. At the end everything is summed up through the introduction, but that seems to have lost its confidence, as if grown weak. It falls to pieces, in order to disappear in the distance, as if ashamed of the whole composition. As if we went back to the beginning and decided that there is no point in further development. (**Mazurka in C major* op. 24 No. 2)

And here are examples of very "humble" endings, ones that accept their fate. This happens where the introduction is repeated in full at the end, without being shortened or changed. It is a clear sign to the listener that the totality of the composition was produced according to plan and now is the time to close it in the right manner, without superfluous sentimentality or exaggeration. That is the ending of such pieces as *Nocturne in A-flat major* op. 32 No. 2:

or *Waltz in A minor* op. 34 No. 2:

And, finally – perhaps one of the most moving endings – as if closed off halfway, frozen almost before dying out properly, as if it wanting to disappear as quickly and as quietly as possible. This is what happens in the final bars of *Mazurka in A flat major* op. 41 No. 4. Is it suspended or embarrassed? Or perhaps it has been frightened off – or just an ordinary withdrawal, a return to one's own place. It seems like an expression of great humility.

Before ending, it is appropriate to know how to end. But what does it mean in practice? What can we learn in this respect from Chopin's music which has just been presented? What is concerned is the very ordinary, mundane practice of the ability to close, simply to finish various matters, from the greatest to the simplest. Nothing lasts forever, nothing is the most important. We hear in this an echo of the comments made a few pages ago – about the necessity of keeping one's distance. Is not such a tactic, paradoxically, the best preparation for death (however this might sound)? After all, every day we come across many opportunities for a good and stylish ending – from looks, through gestures, words and conversations to concrete actions. Behind everything there is precision and responsibility. But hidden even deeper here is our awareness of who we are – what we should do, what the limits of our capabilities are, our acceptance of the necessity of ending and the readiness to take up the challenges that follow from this. The listener's sensitivity is here a prologue to a sensitivity that is much wider and more important – one which allows us fully to perceive and evaluate the existential situation in which we find ourselves, with all its fragility and fleetingness, i.e., the inevitability of it being directed towards the end. If such an attitude permeates our actions, perhaps there will be in them something of Chopin's expressiveness – closeness to another person, the comfort and the intuition that there must be a reality other than the earthly one.

An awareness and acceptance of the necessity of death leads us a step further – towards coming to terms with death. Clearly, it is not a question of being obsessed, but of drawing the furthest possible conclusions from the attitude of distance, i.e., detachment from that which is changeable and transient. In a sense, it is in exactly that manner that one can break down death into various forms of getting rid of attachments, the effort of sharing with others that which is ours. Every time we declare ourselves on the side of what is not ours – and thus has a chance to go beyond us, to survive us – we go through a form of death, or at least its antechamber. This is because we are seeking that which is significant, a point to anchor to, realising well that we cannot count on ourselves to any great degree. In this way we try to cheat – or, at best, get around – the transience of our life. Undoubtedly we want live by that which is important, and not just skin-deep. That is why we are so open to tradition, and to other people. That, however, demands constant sensitivity and is associated with risk. The mysterious vow *conversatio morum* made by the Benedictines means just that kind of constant entering into the unknown. And thus, to a degree, a systematic giving oneself up to death. From the eschatological point of view, such a prospect seems safer than the feeling of safety "at home in oneself". That is the attitude of the "unprofitable servant" (Luke 17, 10), making no claim to gratitude, ready to do the work and leave, making space for others and not getting in the way when one's work has been done. How difficult this is, but what superb style! Everyone has a place, their tasks to perform. When one has succeeded in achieving one's goal, one has to be able to look to what happens next – to us, to our place. In this spirit, one should constantly remind oneself of the words of St Benedict, describing the sixth and seventh degrees of humility:

> *The sixth degree of humility is, when a monk is content with the meanest and worst of everything, and in all that is enjoined him holdeth himself as a bad and worthless workman, saying with the Prophet: "I am brought to nothing and I knew it not; I am become as a beast before Thee, and I am always with Thee" (Ps 72[73]:22–23).*
>
> *The seventh degree of humility is, when, not only with his tongue he declareth, but also in his inmost soul believeth, that he is the lowest and vilest of men, humbling himself and saying with the Prophet: "But I am a worm and no man, the reproach of men and the outcast of the people" (Ps 21[22]:7).* (RulBen 7, 61–68).

Paradoxically, this is the optimal space of trust and safety, always a good ending, a sign of transparency and a deep understanding of what being on this earth is about. When we were born, nobody had asked us whether we wanted to enter this world. We will also die whether we want to or not. This is worth remembering in times of difficulties with relationships. Our little cry is as authentic and important as all of Chopin's works. After all, when nothing is left of this world, his music will share the fate of all human fleetingness. However, both every form of our expression, and Chopin's music, remain an authentic expression of longing and a presentiment of Transcendence. Each of us has an important mission to accomplish. Chopin's music may help us in fulfilling it, like a travelling companion. But it will not take the place of our life…

In order to finish these deliberations which, in sum, treat of things final, one should probably reach for Chopin's *Funeral March*. This, however, would be too literal or banal, all the more so since, in spite of all the splendour of that March, we should remember that it is not the last section of *Piano sonata No.1 in B flat minor* op. 35. There is nothing new in that, we already find that situation in the works of Beethoven, who introduced funeral marches into his sonata (op. 26) and symphonic (op. 55) cycles, where they constitute the middle movements. The last movement of Chopin's *Sonata in B flat minor*, which comes immediately after the *Funeral March*, gives one pause for thought. Much has been written about it, but it keeps attracting attention. One may try to analyse it, but its essence always escapes verbal categories. There are no melodies or characteristic motifs in this short work. Everything is movement, a nebula – and when one listens it is difficult to find anything to lean on, to hold on to. You might have the impression that this is pure motion, but created out of emotions, what you might call "post-funereal" reflections, expressing as much pain as faith, or even a struggle with it. There are in this music both effort and ease, fear and longing. And perhaps that is the same as our approach to death, which may become a portal – and may it be so. (**Piano sonata No. 1 in B flat minor* op. 35. Finale)

The Coda: On the Waves of The World – A Meditation on Benedictine Life Today

One particularly relevant point shared by the music of Chopin and the Benedictine tradition is the fact that each is a minority. Even though these two realities are an inescapable part of the spiritual heritage and of the world (each, of course, in its own way), in practice the number of people who make a serious commitment to them, on a world scale, is small. These are tens, at best hundreds of thousands of people. The number of Benedictine friars and nuns in the world is at present only around 25,000. Oblates and people associated with Benedictine monasteries might be ten times that number. People who play Chopin's music – there may be thousands of those. Undoubtedly there are many more who listen to it, but they are certainly not counted in millions, as in the case of pop music. Does this signify a degree of elitism? Probably. It is no use pretending: these two spheres of spiritual values are not for everyone – they demand a particular attitude: effort, preparation, the right kind of sensitivity. Chopin's music and St Benedict's *Rule* are thus faithful companions in sharing the choice of being in a minority. In the perspective of global interests, and the activity of the world as a whole, this is in fact a tiny drop. Yes, if one takes account of the historical perspective, it has acted as a leaven. Who among the statistical inhabitants of our planet knows who the Benedictines are? Who (outside Poland) will recognise the music of Chopin? Yet no one doubts that both these realities represent a great value – or at least, no one among the readers of these deliberations.

Chopin's music and Benedictine monasticism are thus linked by representing something exotic in the contemporary world. They are both something chosen, sophisticated, not accessible to everyone. The masses, the majority, live by different values, whether we like it or not. Metaphorically speaking, we might thus be on a barge on the waves of the world, carried by various currents and blown about by various winds. The barge is small but, so far, it manages to stay afloat, sailing after its own fashion, righting itself time and again after each buffeting. There is in it a kind of rhythm and a touching dignity. A small piece of the world, rocking in an element so different from itself, that of the whole world. In order to accept such a situation one has to be humble, one has to rid oneself of aspirations concerning majority and domination. One has to concentrate on the present, looking boldly into the future, without constantly circling around the glorious past. That is difficult. Sometimes we would perhaps prefer to be on the side of the elemental waves, instead of quaking with fear on the deck. However, illusion is always a serious threat to spiritual values, including monastic ones; it is thus better to persevere in humming a gondolier's song and bravely steering one's barge than to fall into the temptation of entrusting oneself to the waves. Being faithful to the music of Chopin, as well as to monastic ideals, means to agree to being enclosed in a limited space, always exposed to the danger of annihilation. The Benedictines have always been in the avant-garde, carried by various waves of history. That is, perhaps, the role of all non-institutional – or, rather, charismatic – movements; a dialogue with the unpredictable reality of the world, its richness and complexity. One might say that Chopin's music is also such a small barge, tossed, out of nowhere, onto the ocean of various trends and possibilities of musical expression, which somehow, and for reasons unknown, keeps afloat and bravely sails forth. Being aware of this state of affairs allows one to adopt the right method for enduring, or, more precisely, staying afloat. This is perhaps the best description of the condition of all minorities which do not claim any rights or entitlements to increasing the scope of their influence, but simply want to preserve their own status.

Again, this is a question of both responsibility and patience. The main thing is to stay the course. Some inventiveness, an instinct that finds a way of staying afloat, are essential. This applies both to the Benedictine tradition and to Chopin's music; it is the ability to weave the essence of one's identity into the current reality – and more than that, using that reality to stay afloat and steer the right course. There is nothing more difficult than staying classical in a swiftly flowing current of contemporaneity, when the momentum of life may wash away values that are fragile and defenceless. In such a situation, a strong belief in one's own value, preceded by an unshakeable knowledge of one's own identity, must translate into bravery and a bold vision of one's actions. For this reason the Benedictines – whether they wanted to or not – were the authors of various inventions and solutions which affected civilisation, moving forward economic, cultural and social development. They initiated processes and changes which would later affect themselves as well. Such a challenge is faced by all values of the highest rank. It is not enough that they exist. They must be protected, and that is best done by investing in them by constantly bringing them up to date. This is what steering the right course is, in spite of the varying motion of the waves. It means that Benedictines engage in social, economic and cultural life – of course, in the ways that are open to them. This is possible, and it should be done, at various levels and to varying extent. Such has been the case since the beginnings of monasticism. The first monks in Egypt hired themselves out for public works in order to earn a living. Today, however, what is offered by monasteries is very much sought after, and enjoys much trust, becoming thus a place for the transmission of the most important Christian values. This is a paradox, but also an opportunity both for the contemporary world and the Benedictines. In this way they will not drown in the sea of the modern world – but also that world itself will not lose its points of reference. An openness and creativity that correspond to this interaction are thus not so much a condition of co-existence, as an essential element of the identity and development of both realities. These comments apply also to the music of Chopin. Yes, the world could exist without it: but would it not then lose something important?

Thrown into the element of the waves in our tiny barge, we are thus participants in a great cause – as if a counterpoint to the world, a sign of opposition. By this confrontation we make not only ourselves, but also that world, trustworthy. If thus the Benedictines – or Chopin's music – may achieve something in the world, if they might even change it, they have to do it from the position of an outsider, from their little barge, which undoubtedly is somewhat uncomfortable, but also has a certain charm of its own.

During his stay on Majorca, Chopin composed a number of works which convey very well (and in a unique manner, only possible for Chopin) the play of the waves, being lost in them and their undulating motion at the same time. We find there echoes of sailors' singing, impressions of a sea journey, and an almost tangible impression of bracing sea air carried by sun-soaked breezes. This is what *Nocturne in G major* op. 37 No. 2 is like, gently rocking from its very beginning. Its main theme also undulates, glimpsed in small phrases which gather into a wider arc of melody only after a time. In the narration of this nocturne there is, however, much freedom: as if, carried by the waves we were constantly being tossed and placed in different positions, with our total acceptance of it – in fact, moving along the surface of the water in just such a way. The phrases of this music seem to rise up and fall immediately, only to rise again and fall again. The accompaniment provides a regular rhythm. The melody, in thirds, is only an illustration of what is happening on the surface of the undulating waves, shimmering with various reflections of the sun and shades of colour. The contrasting segment brings, according to tradition, a quotation from a sailors' song – also rhythmical but full of yearning as well. Its motifs, too, in ever-changing tonalities, give the impression of constant rising and rocking on the waves. (**Nocturne in G major* op. 37 No. 2)

Yet another "story" about water and waves is contained in *Ballade No. 2 in F major* op. 38. The opus number locates it immediately after the nocturne discussed above. Here, too, from the very beginning, we hear the undulating rhythm – perhaps more focused than in the nocturne – giving the impression of the water being calmer, almost still. The next segment brings a strong contrast, a kind of exploding cascades or turbulent waves. The water pours over, drops scatter widely on the breeze, glittering in the sun. In this violent motion there is also a strange rhythm of rising and falling, extreme deflections, but also the constant, almost unbelievable floating on the surface. (*Ballade No. 2 in F major* op. 38)

The element of water, a sea journey, is always located between two extremes: water is either calm or turbulent. In life we have to make a number of journeys of this kind. In fact, we make them all the time. We are always emerging from our isolation towards being with other people; from inner concentration to taking on projects, sometimes very large ones that are beyond us; from closed circles in which we live to the open structures of modern society. These crossings between the two realities are like travelling across the waves. And also, the fact that we have entered a particular reality and want to stay there does not protect us from the dangers of the journey. All our actions in time presuppose the necessity of moving between different contexts and dimensions. This poses a constant threat to that which is the most important, but also offers the possibility of making it stronger: constant alertness and care, an always present sense of responsibility.

The ambiguity of the turbulent flow is also an integral part of the journey described here. That is the case, for instance, with our civilisation. Whether we want to or not, we are immersed in what might perhaps be better described as problematic and absorbing convulsions rather than turbulent waves. In a large measure, however, we float carried by these waves. The network of communications and economics, of various demesnes and relationships, feels like a bottomless, sometimes very turbulent ocean. But we live in it, sometimes cheating on the tight space of our barge. How is one to stay true to its course? The point is not to be carried by the waves, but to sail in a particular direction. This means taking great care of one's barge and the uncomfortable loneliness squeezed into it. It is a choice of constant risk and a fragile feeling of safety. That is how we might describe the ever-present tension in Benedictine life between constancy and conversion – between the silence of concentration and the dynamism of action. The righteous living through this tension is a condition of achieving a proper balance, the Benedictine moderation in the space of our life. Achieving and maintaining that balance is the most difficult thing in Benedictine life. The metaphor of a barge sailing on turbulent waves, which we have been analysing here, conveys this situation very well. Nothing can be settled. There is no peace. And yet, as we have said, that is what the space of our relationships, activities and life projects is like. This balance also ensures silence, solitude and peace. It has to be achieved, and once that happens, one has to be fully alert to protect it.

There is one more dimension to sailing in a barge, we might call it the inner one. That is our own commitment in relation to sailing itself, to steering the course and remaining afloat. This is the inner alertness which makes it possible to steer the barge effectively. There is a danger of becoming so involved in the voyage, so delighted with the surrounding nature, that one loses control of the barge. Betraying moderation may bring annihilation. Although these days the extreme "either-or" attitudes are very often dominant, the ability to maintain the right balance is crucial. One might thus follow Father Piotr Rostworowski in saying that, in the well-known Benedictine maxim *ora et labora*, it is the *et* that is the hardest thing to achieve. This is the difficulty of the unstable limited space of the barge and its always uncomfortable position. All that is left is the rhythm, its comforting consistency, expressing some kind of solidarity with the water – with the whole world. It should live, pulsate, rock, and thus enable us to clear our path. Following the Egyptian monks, this should mean being faithful to the monastic ideal, as well as true involvement in social life at the same time, even if in principle monks live separated from the world. The image returns here of a barge rolling on the waves, with its conflicting messages of being at home and entrusting oneself, remaining afloat and the constant threat of being swallowed by the abyss. This creates the paradoxical dialectic of being at rest in motion, and motion through rest, corresponding to the typical Benedictine binomial "constancy-conversion". If we add to this binomial the vow of obedience, the question of the direction in which the barge is sailing becomes clear. Fortunately, we are not steering it by ourselves. Our image turns out to be strongly evangelical: the motif of a boat sailing a turbulent lake, and the tension arising out of the presence or absence of Christ, turn out to be some of the key icons of the revelation of God in the New Testament. This makes it that much easier to transfer them to Benedictine life, and our life in general.

All these threads are gathered together in a singular piece by Chopin. As they sum up our existential situation, so this composition provides, to some extent, a synthesis of the expression of Chopin's music. This is his *Barcarolle in F-sharp major* op. 60 – a kind of apotheosis of multidimensional rocking on the waves. A lot more could be said about this work but, in the context of what has already been said above, the work speaks for itself. What is most significant in it is the ubiquitous presence of the rhythm of motion on a wave, which takes on different forms. It tells of things that are most important, yet remains close to the heart of every listener. Interpreting this image in terms of the present situation of the Benedictines in the world, we see first of all the necessity of constantly linking it to the evangelical stories of sailing on water, of Jesus walking on the waves, and the mysterious tension between these two ways of experiencing the waves. We need only to remind ourselves of Peter's attempt to walk on the waves, as well as Jesus calming the waves and crossing from the lake to the boat. It brings to mind a description formulated by Elmar Salmann, a Benedictine theologian and philosopher, and a penetrating observer and witness of modern changes. He defined his role – that of a monk and theologian – as a "humble ferryman between worlds"[20]. This description very vividly complements the images recalled earlier. It also indicates just how multifaceted is the metaphor of sailing a barge on turbulent seas, combining both spiritual and existential experiences. This is what also happens in the *Barcarolle*: alongside the multi-level undulations of the rhythm, we find there melodies of diverse format – single-threaded, but also shimmering with a multitude of threads which grow out of them. They intensify, they develop, the whole work is like one great "sailing", with a well-defined course, consciously accepting its consequences. It is also a study in motion and space, rhythm and liberation. At the same time, the music touches only lightly on that which is most important to everyone of us. It leads us and invites us to find that motion and the harmony of its rhythm in the varied situations of our life. (**Barcarolle in F-sharp major* op. 60)

---

[20] E. Salmann, *Być pokornym przewoźnikiem między światami*, [in:] by the same author, *Daleka bliskość chrześcijaństwa*, transl. into Polish B. Sawicki, Kraków 2005, pp. 277–314.

Ps: The Aporias of Chopin's Music – The *Rule* is Only the Beginning

Probably in a presentation of any subject there comes a moment when we reach a boundary – not so much that there is nothing more to be said, as that there is a need to leave space for a true and personal contact between the recipient of a given presentation and the subject itself. Every description is a form of mediation, which needs to accept its own limits and inadequacy, a difficult task when perfectionism (or professionalism) and pragmatism are the dominant values. Philosophy has a concept which describes just such an inability: *aporia* is the place which cannot be defined, which escapes the system. It is not necessarily equivalent to straying into the wilderness in a discourse, but, rather, means that the adequacy of the formula used so far has been exhausted, and suggests that it should be modified in order to correspond more closely to reality (this does not mean that it will not need to be changed again in a while). Aporia is a concrete, sometimes painful – whether expected or not – entry into the area of doubt. This is a problem, but also an opportunity. In a discussion of the spiritual, or even mystical aspects of Chopin's music, the concept of *aporia* may be of great significance. If by a spiritual experience we understand something that goes beyond matter, beyond the finite, yet of necessity remains associated with it in some way, *a priori* or *a posteriori, aporia* would be the moment of separation from the limits of matter, finiteness and controllability. This implies helplessness, confrontation or conflict, but also a moving on, an experience of transcendence, entry into a sphere that is unknown and perhaps frightening, but doing so constructively and with hope. How can this happen in the case of Chopin's music? How can this make a mark on our experience of it?

In order to answer this question let us draw attention to the fact that Chopin created a virtually perfect system of expression which, in a way, is closed; it is also recognisable, rich and comprehensible. This is the impression one might gain from a general acquaintance with his music. In the words of Przybylski: "music was speech to him – speech which uses indefinite words or sounds not burdened with music. It is thus communication beyond the verbal."[21] It seems to be something different, something that perhaps goes further than speech but, like speech,

---

21 R. Przybylski, *Cień jaskółki*, p. 237.

it is systemically defined.[22] However, Chopin's works contain, not numerous in total but still present, places which indicate that this system is inadequate. As has been noted by Przybylski, one might get the impression that the composer is being torn by the need for expression, since "the sound which constitutes the essence of an 'undefined word' cannot be linked to any meaning".[23] What Chopin wants to transmit, that supra-musical content, is richer and stronger than the most sophisticated structures and configurations of Chopinian forms. We thus have in Chopin's music, at the very centre of its shaping, places which are open, not fully defined – like a horizon, the ultimate perspective on what is made possible by music. It is difficult to say whether these places express conscious restraint, or whether they testify to helplessness on having reached the limit. We do not know whether they are a consequence of the logic of the creative system, or the effect of some mysterious external inspiration. Perhaps an alternative solution was available; but it is also possible that there was no other choice. At these points we seem to reach the end of music and the boundaries of its language – so varied, as we know, depending on the period and the place. It is not surprising that these places, purposely or not, act as precursors in the perspective of the history of music. They express an intuition about what could happen further on, about the new, unknown horizons, and that is why they are so close to mysticism. They push beyond the sphere of that which can be encompassed, that which is known consciously and which can be controlled. However, they are not amorphous. They do indicate a course, even though it is being sought blindly. Because of that they have something prophetic about them. They testify to the touch of the inexpressible – through that which is inexpressible.

Most often situations of this kind arise at the end of compositions, at the cadences or before them. It is as if the stock of devices available in the work has been exhausted, yet something still remains to be transmitted. Or as if a need arose to surprise again the listener who has become accustomed to (not to say tired of) the flow of the composition. At some point attention dwindles and has to be stimulated again, or allowed to rest. In the classical sonata form the cadence at the end of the movement was also an opportunity for the performer to present a display of virtuosity. Chopin turned cadences into a pretext for a particular expressiveness, often very far from that which was used throughout in the

---

22   "Music is autonomous speech which transports human thought into a sphere of abstraction impossible to lexicalise, although, like all speech, it has its own logic, i.e. rules governing the expression of thought", ibid., p. 247.
23   Ibid. p. 240.

composition. This is what happens in the last segment of *Nocturne in H major* op. 32 No. 1. Before the arrival of the definitive ending, the division into bars seems to be blurred. In place of the narration regularly measured by the pulsation of the metre, we have free recitative. The discourse of the work seems to have lost its way or got stuck. For just a moment, but a very telling one, regardless of whether we ask: *why?* or whether we accept the situation as a natural consequence of the logic of the composition, we remain disturbed in some way. The regular flow of the composition taking place so far has, in a sense, been undermined.

Just as in the above example one might talk about "dilution" of expression, *Prelude in C-sharp minor* op. 45 brings a "densification" in its ending. This composition, very cohesive in terms of expression, conveys the persistent intensity of the movement of emotion in a very suggestive and at the same time restrained manner; however, with the arrival of the cadence, the narration not only breaks down, but seems to intensify. Constantly modulated chromatics become maximally concentrated, without, however, going beyond Chopin's natural restraint, always far removed from emotionalism. There is in it a conscious, controlled obsession, almost entering the space of pure emotion.

The cadence of the second movement of *Piano concerto No. 1 in E minor* op. 11, *Romanza*, goes further along these lines. Here, too, the earlier narration is shattered into scattering, chromatically saturated two-note motifs. It is as if the enchantment of a moonlit night suddenly became a luminous, pulsating aura that is not of this world, full of mystery, unlike anything else, eluding all attempts at a description.

The previous musical discourse is permanently deformed. The final phrases of this movement of the concerto, which result directly from the cadence, bring a totally different motion – measured, but denser, yet much toned down by the cadence in terms of expressiveness. The melody seems to cascade, acting as a whole, as a line or even a plane, while in the cadence the notes were grouped as points. In this way, taking into account the whole previous arrangement of *Romanza* which, generally speaking, followed the classical model, the listener is taken beyond the melody, or perhaps towards its horizon; it dissolves in some proto-pulsation, leaving in a pure state the most private movements of our emotions and our spirit. There was no indication that the basic discourse of this movement would lead to something like that. Both the cadence and the coda, in a sense, go beyond the listener's original expectations, and do so in such a direction that the latter feels enchanted by the new perspective which suddenly appears ahead. Perhaps that was what the composer felt as well.

Aporia is thus a way of opening. At the same time, and this should be clearly stated, it is a gap (a lack) in a system, an inadequacy of what has gone before. This is an important moment in dialectic opening. Aporia turns out to be an opportunity for a new quality, a new level of expression or understanding. Amorphous on the one hand, on the other it is a new shape. It moves the original expression of the composition onto new tracks. One of its very moving examples is Chopin's amazing tendency to literalism, perhaps even naturalism. It conflicts with his other tendency, towards restraint and certain objectivism of expression which we mentioned earlier. But this intensifies even more the effect of going beyond the system, a procedure that testifies to a degree of determination, masked by the tangible closeness, the shadow of the system. More precisely: a system is a formula of expression which provides the basic framework for the discourse of a composition. In a majority of compositions, expression is achieved using the same means which are defined and presented at the beginning. A formula thus created is basically predictable. Aporia, in our understanding, involves breaking down, or extending, this formula. This event is so powerful, and so difficult to explain in terms of the original categories adopted in the composition, that it becomes a new quality; one, however, which is not capable of shaping a new formula. It is ephemeral, more of a sign, an indication of something beyond.

To return to Chopin's "literalism", we see it in such a sharpening, such a direct presentation of expression that it reaches the boundaries of what constitutes music, almost touching physiology or realism. This, in a sense, is the character of *Prelude in F minor* op. 28 No. 18. The strong contrasting of two basic threads of expression – unison runs of sixteenths and chordal parts, at times distributed within a wide ambitus – brings to mind some kind of extremes of expressiveness. The music, and Chopin's restraint, seem to have difficulty coping with the violence and power of the emotions they are transmitting. It seems difficult to model, or to combine them appropriately. The narration seems to be overburdened with the almost somatic pressure of the sound material. At one point we seem to be dealing with convulsiveness, or even explosiveness, rather than a systematic development of form. The music no longer pretends that it wants to mediate. It lets us really touch the pain and helplessness of people, or of life – perhaps even unconsciously becoming a record of the symptoms of a disease…? (**Prelude in F minor* op. 28 No. 18)

Preludes, being small forms, frequently provide examples of such an approach to musical expression, paradoxically un-Chopinian in its atypicality. *Prelude in E-flat minor* op. 28 No. 14 is amorphous in a different sense from the one discussed earlier. The unison narration, quite compact and turbulent at the same time, seems to be a record of pure emotion, its movements not fully coordinated and conscious. It appears to be a pure, raw idea, a pre-reflective transmission, as yet far from having tackled the issue of its own form – expression *in statu nascendi*, yet very authentic, reaching to the deepest, and thus most elusive movements of the heart; what might be described as an X-ray of a moment of experience. (**Prelude in E-flat minor* op. 28 No. 14)

It sometimes happens that an emotion, long imprisoned in a regularly planned and controlled form, will not be able to take it to the end and will pour out, or even explode. These are "pointilistic" aporias, particularly difficult to reconcile with the Chopinian stylistics. The intricate and constant composing of the form's network is, for a moment, frayed, or even torn. The agitation, the anger, seem to go beyond the limits of good taste. Victory goes to the obsessiveness that wants to scream itself out through insistent repetition of some kind. Usually this happens at the end of the larger forms – in the culminating crisis of a cadence, of which the most emphatic example is the dissonant chord at the very end of *Scherzo No. 1 in B minor* op. 20, repeated nine times. That crisis, in the words of Jarosław Iwaszkiewicz "affects us so strongly, and must have evoked cries of indignation in the ladies, and the shrugging of shoulders in the gentlemen, in the salons of Vienna and Paris"[24].

Similar "throwing oneself about" come at the final crisis of the expression both in *Scherzo No. 2 in B minor* op. 31:

---

24 J. Iwaszkiewicz, *Pisma muzyczne. Chopin*, Warszawa 1958, p. 391.

and in *Fantasia in F minor* op. 49:

For a moment, all the proprieties are broken, a cry sounds out in great agitation, and impatience itself takes over the steering of the narration for a moment that is brief, yet leaves a definite mark on the heart.

There may be different varieties of this phenomenon. Sometimes it might appear that the Chopinian aporia becomes, after all, a principle which regulates the parameters of expression in a longer segment of a composition. Here also the intensity of emotional saturation reaches its peak. However, appropriately prepared for and conducted, it may for a time become the norm for itself. This is precisely what happens in the middle part of *Etude in E major* op. 10 No. 3, otherwise essentially "nocturnal" in nature. Here, the cascading sixths running down diminished chords are prepared for by the gradual rising of motifs with just such a texture, which break through the previous narration – in itself more turbulent than the initial one – with increasing effectiveness. In the climax it seems as if something had burst. Cascades of sixths, pulsating in various ways and in various directions, keep falling in an unbroken stream which rises and falls – but nothing can stop its insistent flow. The healing return of the initial motif of "regret", mentioned earlier in relation to this etude, is all the more effective. (*Etude in E major* op. 10 No. 3)

One could, and probably should, ask about the significance of these aporias, since we can see their various dimensions and forms, as if pushing their way into Chopin's classical discourse, picking out cracks and nesting in them. Are they parasites, or an opportunity to see the real face of musical expression, i.e. the reality which hides behind it? Aporia both intrigues and misleads. Most often it wants to remain unobserved. When noticed, it tries to mislead the observer, deprecating its role. It is an opportunity to avoid becoming "looped into" just the music itself. It allows us the hope of opening music up not so much to life, as to its mystery – to the clues which lead towards Transcendence. It pulls us out of the lethargy of competent craftsmanship and erudition, thus ensuring that music has a life that is authentic, unpredictable and inexplicable, which undoubtedly carries a deeper message within it.

Having defined a little more clearly the semantic field of aporia, we may try and show its functioning on a wider scale, i.e., where its presence marks more extended fragments of musical narration in the larger forms. This is what clearly happens in *Polonaise in F-sharp minor* op. 44. Its basic profile is drawn decisively from the very beginning. There is no doubt as to its both heroic and triumphal character. This is the music of a splendid national epopee, and the episode based on motifs of rising Dorian scale retains this character. Everything is planned and developed with a vigour that leaves no doubts or uncertainties. It seems impossible to hold back this energy. And then, when the full presentation of the material of the first part of this "polonaise *par excellence*" has been completed, there appears a very strange bridging episode. It might be described as amorphous, although Chopin develops and conducts it with a certain logic which seems stronger than the material it is trying to organise. The rhythm and the distinct motifs – something like the stamping, beating – of feet? hooves? – intrigues by its intensifying determination. In order to tone it down, Chopin brings in an expressive motif of the ascending Dorian scale, something in the nature of a sigh. But then the amorphic convulsions, or clouds of thirty-seconds, broken through by octaves in eighths, make their return.

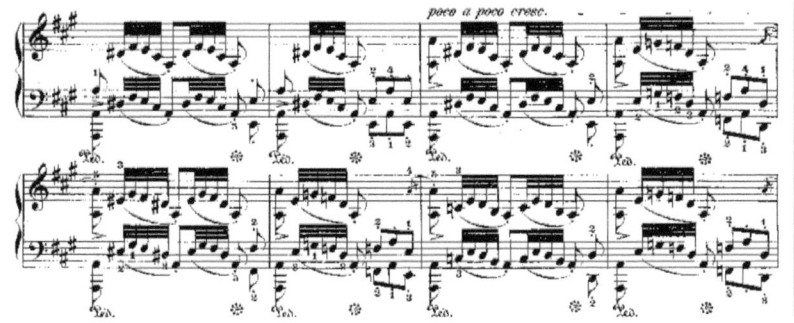

It is difficult to say anything about this fragment. Its mobility and vitalism are far removed from the nobility so typical of Chopin. Its obsessive nature seems to do violence to his usual moderation. It sounds like the aggressive, vitalistic piano compositions written a hundred years later. And yet we feel that it could not have been any other way. Surprised, perhaps a little shocked, we allow ourselves to be led by this music, even though we do not know where to. But, in truth, everything is known and has been prepared in advance. The aporia of this bridge is unequivocal in leading nowhere else but to a revelation. When we allow it to take charge of us, we suddenly find ourselves in a country with quite different poetics. The mystery, and the greatest attribute of this polonaise, is Chopin's introduction, in the middle part, of an ordinary mazurka. Ordinary and shocking, since it is found at the end of a path which eludes any musical control. This is how aporia breaks and solves itself. As if it was trying to show that it is both necessary and subservient. It presents new perspectives on what until then had been understood by the concept of a polonaise. With generous hospitality it accepts all our awkwardness and helplessness, embarrassment in the face of heroism and greatness, melting them discreetly and gracefully into our most timid longings and dreams – of happiness, and of Poland. The aporia in question turns out here to be a bridge between the heroic and the idyllic, between the high tone of that which is national and the enchanting and lost innocence. In this, it is both natural and surprising, discreet and consistent.

Following this trail we reach a composition the climax of which is aporic, *Ballade in F minor* op. 52 (which has been mentioned previously). Its character is variational. The theme of these variations undergoes consecutive metamorphoses, which consistently intensify its expressiveness in a very suggestive and sophisticated manner. The whole narration is characterised by continuous and steadfast intensification. But this time, too, the inner power of the music, or some mysterious external imperative driving Chopin, imparts a surprising, aporic shape to the climax. At a particular point – theoretically the most appropriate one for its resolution – the successively intensifying expressiveness breaks down. This produces the effect of expectation and suspension, but at the same time seems to foreshadow a totally new quality in the discourse of the composition, and this is what actually takes place. The segment which appears after the chordal section of slowing down surprises with its untamed nature and the density and complexity of texture. Everything seems to be boiling, billowing. At times one or another motif emerges on the surface for a moment. Basically, however, we still have the impression of some deep convulsiveness, which does not in any way fit in with the sophistication of the work so far. Did something break? Not enough patience and devices? No, that would not be possible with Chopin! And this time also we feel that it could not have been otherwise. Our embarrassment is strangely interwoven with relief. The tension brought about by being tied to the sophisticated development of the form could not be borne any more. That is why everything had to fall to pieces, and immediately rise and explode. Aporia is so human because it disarms the system, not allowing it to grow to dimensions which would oppress us. It is an expression of pity, as well as understanding and goodwill towards our inadequacy. Truly we need it as we need our breath, and our need grows as we wander through the spaces of the greatest art. It reminds us of the deepest meaning of art, which is beyond art and which, to be reached, demands that, in a sense, we destroy, annihilate art – or save it through aporia. (*)

Our deliberations cannot end otherwise than by referring to what is perhaps the most mysterious of Chopin's works, one which has also been mentioned earlier. This is the

Finale from *Piano sonata No. 1 in B minor* op. 35. That composition closes the four-movement sonata cycle, the culminaton of which is the third movement, the *Funeral march*. Such arrangement of the sonata cycle was not an idea which originated with Chopin; Beethoven used it before him, first in his *Piano sonata in A-flat major* op. 26, and then also in his *Symphony No. 3 in E-flat major* op. 55. We described Chopin's composition as having a mysterious form of ending, one without precedent. In order to widen the scope of our earlier reflections on this subject, let us note the paradoxical nature of the composition in question. From the psychological point of view, the ending undoubtedly brings a relaxation of tension, totally discharging the formal and textural tension relating to the *Funeral march.* This "discharge", however, means that in fact the form is diluted, not to say washed away. It seems to be served, as it were, in one throw. We have difficulty distinguishing any segments in it, whereas in the preceding *Funeral march* this was one of the main principles of shaping the form. It would also be difficult to talk about the harmonic component of the form – the *Finale* is in unison throughout, with harmonic traces in the diachronic dimension. However, the melody served to us has an amorphous character. It is difficult to perceive it in a linear aspect; it creates more of an impression of a cloud or a vibrating swarm. Motion with a nebulous character, staticity that is pulsating internally – these are the two textural and expressive poles of this work that complement each other. The question about the reasons for such expression at exactly this point in the sonata, even though frequently asked, must remain without an answer. Just as it was difficult for us to imagine this sonata with a different ending, so it remains a puzzle – perhaps the most distinctive and intriguing among Chopin's aporias; important enough to still carry in it an unresolved mystery, accessible enough to form a whole part of a cycle. In this case, too, we feel that Chopin is entering new, unknown horizons with his music. Has anyone, though, gone further along this path, or is it simply that a door to some other reality was slightly opened…? Did the pressure of the whole form of the cycle turn out to be too great, or did the form – and its proper conclusion – stop having any meaning at that point? (*)

A Hypothetical Ending: On the Other Side

Whatever we might say, both about the music of Chopin and the *Rule* of St Benedict, and whatever we might not say, they live on because of us, the debtors and depositaries of dead geniuses. Theoretically one might imagine that, in a while, when a cataclysmic event strikes or our culture comes to an end, both Chopin's music and St Benedict's teachings will disappear without trace. This means that there will simply be no people committed to and involved in living their work – which, parenthetically, can come to pass without a cataclysmic event of any kind.

So far, both works "are doing well", still filling and fulfilling the lives of thousands or even millions of people, and bearing new and amazing fruit, not only in people's hearts. And that is amazing, that the work of one particular person should have such an enormous power of influence. After all, St Benedict has been gone from us for nearly fifteen centuries, and Chopin for over one and a half. Perhaps we should say that they have ensured immortality for themselves. Yes and no. Their earthly life ended, as happens with every human life. If they have survived, it is in their work. How great then must be its power! And how important the personalities of the authors who left their mark on the work, whether we regard this as a privilege or something obvious. And at the same time one gets the feeling that the Benedictine tradition did not arise by accident, just as Chopin's music was not created by accident. If not by accident – does this mean that they had – and have – a role to play? What role? Presumably sufficiently important for them to live on and develop many years after the death of their creators. But what about them themselves? Are they still important, or did their role come to an end when their work entered the world? Is the work then more important than they? And they – are they to fade from memory sooner than their work? Even though it came from them? And can we believe that one day there will be no Benedictines and no music by Chopin? Our intuition of eternity becomes very focused and active when faced with the most important values. It carries with it not only the question about the meaning and purpose of human life, but also about the human right to eternity. Not every one of us is a St Benedict, or a Chopin, but as their work goes beyond the dimension of their life, the life of each one of us wants to reach further than the prospect of this earthly life. Both the Benedictine tradition and Chopin's music seem to offer a powerful confirmation of this. More than that: their existence and development confirm also the existence and importance of a personal, intimate bond with values which transcend the death of their creators. Perhaps this bond is the best guarantee and form of their immortality? Through it, each of us establishes a personal and unique contact with St Benedict or with Chopin's music. There are no omniscient experts here. Everyone's reception, emotion is important. In a sense, brilliant creators become our debtors in this context. We travel together a path that leads somewhere further and higher than temporality. All the more reason not to doubt that both St Benedict and Chopin, like so many great creators and all those who respond to their work, are there together, on the other side, together representing the same cause. It is a kind of ultimate meeting in the infinity, in the space of ultimate fulfilment, unfaltering perfection and everlasting happiness – a return to paradise, to the sources of beauty and humanity – and thus to the sources and the fruit of their work. In the final count, what remains for eternity is that eschatological enduring – beyond time and matter, beyond the changeability of human experiences and moods. There, all the aporias will become clear and, most importantly, we will have, we trust, the same perspective on the past and the future as St Benedict, as Chopin, and as so many other great ones whose work led us along the paths of temporality.

If this is so, let us try to imagine, as far as possible, one of those eschatological meetings "on the other side" – in the world beyond. Trying to imagine this eludes all parameters of fantasy or futurology. Theology cannot capture it either. Perhaps mysticism comes closer to it…? In any case, the aura of mystery and indistinctness present also here justifies us in drawing, through such an attempt, some singular, extreme conclusions regarding that reality that is stretched so tight between that which is God's and that which is human, both in the *Rule* of St Benedict, and the music of Chopin. And so…

"It's interesting, how long we have been sitting here together listening to that singing coming from nearby. Many have come and gone – you remain. Who are you? I seem to know you…"

"All of us here know each other from somewhere. I am Benedict of Nursia. And this singing is truly extraordinary. Are you a musician?"

"So it turned out. Perhaps now that is not the most important thing. My name is Fryderyk Chopin. Music is everywhere here, but this singing is different somehow. I always felt that the melody is the most important thing, because of its power. But I have never heard a melody as beautiful as this singing."

"That is why I also sit here so often – even though it is true, as you say, that everything all around us is singing. But this singing has in it both depth and simplicity. It has in it truth about life, about humankind, about happiness."

"But also a kind of cheerful anxiety. I know it only too well. It was my inseparable companion when I searched for the final shape of a melody. Here the melody has a shape that is pure and obvious, and that anxiety seems to be there only to find comfort immediately. But because the melody lives – which means it surprises and changes – the anxiety keeps coming back in order to immediately become fulfilment."

"And that is why one can listen to it without end. When I listen I understand all the more what peace is. I searched for it so, and I had a presentiment of it in my heart – in the care for others, in the ordinariness and the order of life – probably as you did in the melodies you composed."

"But, ultimately, you must have felt that it comes from above. And that it needs concentration, sacrifice, withdrawal, if one is not to lose it."

"It is the salvation which lies in silence and in peace." [25]

"This was exactly my impression when I was composing, or rather discovering, melodies. The most profound experience was at the monastery in Majorca. Here I feel that we are at the source of the melody…"

"Undoubtedly – we are at the source of life. It flows, even though its nature is unchanging joy and peace…"

"Every melody on earth had its end. This one keeps on and yet is not tedious, always equally delicate and lively. When I wrote my music I always had to take care that time should not deform it. Here – there is no time."

"We are in eternity. Our feelings and desires find themselves in infinity. *Deep calleth unto deep*[26]. A little like in your music."

"You know it?"

"We all know it here – largely from the time before you wrote it down on earth."

"That's true, I always felt that it did not come from me. I heard it somewhere deep inside – or rather high above. What remained was what I managed to hold on to and preserve. Were you involved in music too?"

"Yes and no. I heard much of it in the silence of the dawn of Subiaco, or in the south on Monte Cassino, pulsating with the heat of the sun. It was where you said – deep inside and above."

"Did you compose?"

"I wouldn't have been able to. There was too much of it. You could not capture and preserve it. The only thing that did not frighten it away was silence – and humility. That is why it only remained in my heart. Then more, new waves of it came in prayer and in the singing of psalms. Irresistible, but always surprising, they washed away the previous ones, which one regretted. Now all that music that I brushed against during prayer and that escaped me, – now I find it here.

---

25 Cf. Isaiah 30,15.
26 Ps 42,8.

"I tried to hold on to what I heard, and note it down. It cost a lot, but I felt that I had to make that effort, that that was my task. The melodies I heard waiting to be discovered were too beautiful and distinct."

"You passed them on to people. You did good."

"I was most afraid of not being able to reproduce that which I heard. And in fact, that which I held on to was only a trace of the pure original. If I succeeded in preserving it, then it must have been good. Here I find it in its full shape – the obvious melody, accessible without the effort of its creator."

"So many generations drew on the good of the music which you wrote down. Many people owe you much."

"That is true. But I cannot take credit for that. This is, rather, an amazing whim of grace. It is only now, when I am close to its source, that I understand why I had to take on the effort of recording and passing on to others the music that I heard."

"*For none of us lives for himself.* [27] Ultimately you also were searching for the peace that is the fruit of love. I am sure it was not easy for you."

"Struggling with the resistant material of music, I was not very good at "struggling" with people. But I did need – and love them, so much! After all, someone did say that beauty is the shape of love."[28]

"And love on earth always had to be accompanied by yearning and lack of fulfilment. You recorded them in music."

"Or rather Someone comforted me with it. And I even wondered what use all that writing of mine would be to people."

"Perhaps you simply wanted to share with people the comfort you received. Serving people, doing good – we ultimately help ourselves."

"Comfort fills loneliness with bonds. I ran away from people to music, which would then bind me to them. In both cases I felt how much love there was in it."

"Because that is how love on earth has to be. Its fragility and its pain testify that it comes from here. There, on earth, it was in exile."

"Like the most beautiful melodies, it was at the mercy of the limitedness of the people who served it and the material which they had to use. But once you heard it in its true shape it brought meaning and gave strength."

"Fortunately here weakness has reached its end. Love, singing and grace in their purest form remain forever the source of adoration and peace. They will never again be accompanied by care, or the pain of unfulfilment."

---

27   Romans 7,1.4.
28   Cf. C.K. Norwid, *Promethidion*, [in:] *Pisma wszystkie*, by the same author, vol. 3, p. 437.

"This is both the end and the beginning of music. I always knew that it carried truth about life. Each time it guarded it jealously, demanding a high price for every secret I tore from it that had to do with that truth."

"You would not give way. Your effectiveness means that you had humility, patience and self-sacrifice. Whether you wanted to or not, you discovered through music the true, Divine face of life. Undoubtedly that is why you are here."

"On earth, God was closest when in hiding. Especially there where I wanted love so much, to the point of seeking it blindly."

"Sincerity in your search was sufficient to find Him. In truth, it is only that – and as much as that – that mattered in life.

"Perhaps that is why life had to be painful. Every search is a risk, unless it is changed by the grace that prompts us towards the right clues. Now we have found and are facing the pure melody. It flows so peacefully, because God is no longer hiding. On earth music was His hiding place."

"Yes and no. He is the singing. In music, He was sometimes closer than in any other form of His concealment. It was – and remains – His closest companion."

"So I was quite lucky. If it were not for music, I would probably have never found Him here. Who knows, perhaps it prevented me from becoming totally lost in being with people."

"Music is grace, that is, a path of salvation. It was not you seeking Him. He was seeking you, and through you – others. He undoubtedly was at the time when you passed on music to others."

"I wonder what was more beautiful – and perhaps also more important: the discovering, the gathering of music in the field of inspirations, or playing it for people. Sometimes I managed to do both. But really these are two sides of the same coin."

"Inasmuch as we have done it unto one of the least of these His brethren, we have done it unto Him.[29] There is no truly beautiful music without people."

"Or without their longings and without their hope of fulfilment."

"That means – without expanding the heart running to paradise.[30] Because music was and is a touch of paradise – both on earth and here. Have you found your music here yet?"

"I never even thought of it. There is so much of it that is more beautiful within reach. Do you think it is somewhere here?"

---

29   Matthew 25,40.
30   Cf. RulBen Prologue, 53.

"It cannot be otherwise because, as I said, it comes from here. It did not return here – it has always been here."

"I wonder – did I succeed in writing it down as it sounds here"

"You will hear. It is now easy to check that which some of the more perceptive authors on earth tried to glimpse – for example, whether the angel choirs praise God with Bach's music but are much more likely to be playing Mozart for themselves, with the good Lord happily eavesdropping.[31] Whatever the case, I am sure you are going to play, and more than once, for Him and for the angels. And they will be just improvisations – the purest ones, from the very source of His grace."

---

31 This is an allusion to the words of K. Barth in his *Dankbrief an Mozart* published on 21 January 1956 in: "Luzerner Neusten Nachrichten". Quoted after: K. Barth, *Wolfgang Amadeus Mozart*, Zürich 2006, p.29

Index of Works by Fryderyk Chopin Referrred to in the Text

An asterisk (*) indicates a recommendation to listen to these works in full. Each composition is mentioned once in the index, although some of them are referred to more than once in the text.

Ballade No. 1 in G minor op. 23 (*)
Fantasia in F-minor op. 49 (*)
Fantasia on Polish Airs in A major op. 13 (*)
Mazurka in F-major op. 68 No. 3 (*)
Etude in C minor op. 10 No. 12 (*)
Impromptu in G-flat major op. 51 (*)
Piano concerto No. 1 in E minor op. 11, 1st movement, Allegro maestoso
Polonaise in A flat major op. 53
Piano concerto in F minor op. 21, 2nd movement, Larghetto
Ballade No. 4 in F minor op. 52
Mazurka in C major op. 7 No. 5 (*)
Waltz in D flat major op. 64 No. 1
Waltz in C sharp minor op. 64 No. 2
Mazurka in C sharp minor op. 41 No. 1
Scherzo No. 3 in C sharp minor op. 37
Barcarolle in F sharp op. 60 (*)
Mazurka in B-flat major op. 7 No.1
Mazurka in E minor op. 41 No. 2
Polonaise in A major op. 40 No. 1
Etude in G-sharp minor op. 25 No. 6 (*)
Piano sonata No. 3 in B minor op. 58, Finale. Presto non tanto (*)
Mazurka in C-sharp minor op. 63 No. 3.
Andante Spianato and Grand Polonaise in E-flat major op. 22 (*)
Mazurka in F minor op. 68 No. 4 (*)
Prelude in C-sharp minor op. 45 (*)
Mazurka in A minor op. 7 No. 2
Prelude in A minor op. 28 No. 2 (*)
Nocturne in G minor op. 15 No. 3 (*)
Nocturne in E major op. 62 No. 2
Mazurka in C-sharp minor op. 50 No. 3

Mazurka in C major op. 56 No. 2.
Nocturne in E flat major op. 55 No. 2 (*)
Etude in A minor op. 25 No. 11
Prelude in D-flat major op. 28 No. 15 (*)
Berceuse in D-flat major op. 57 (*)
Nocturne in B minor op. 9 No.1 (*)
Polonaise in G minor (*)
Mazurka in F-sharp minor op. 6 No. 1 (*)
Nocturne in B major op. 9 No. 3 (*)
Etude in E major op. 10 No. 3 (*)
Scherzo No. 1 in B minor op. 20 1 (*)
Etude in C minor op. 10 No. 12 (*)
Etude in C minor op. 25 No. 12 (*)
Polonaise in F-sharp minor op. 44
Scherzo No. 2 in B minor op. 31 No. 2
Scherzo No. 4 in E major op. 54
Mazurka in A minor op. 17 No. 4
Prelude in E minor op. 28 No. 4 (*)
Grande Valse brillante in E-flat major op. 18 (*)
Prelude in C-sharp minor op. 28 No. 10 (*)
Waltz in A-flat major op. 69 No. 1
Mazurka in A minor op. 67 No. 4
Nocturne in F minor op. 55 No. 1
Fantasie-impromptu in C-sharp minor op. 66 (*)
Etude in E-flat major op.10 No. 11 (*)
Prelude in E-flat major op. 28 No. 19 (*)
Etude in F major op. 10 No. 8
Etude in F major op. 25 No. 3
Mazurka in C major op. 24 No. 2 (*)
Nocturne in A-flat major op. 32 No. 2
Waltz in A minor op. 34 No. 2
Mazurka in A-flat major op. 41 No. 4
Piano sonata No. 1 in B minor op. 35. Finale (*)
Nocturne in G major op. 37 No. 2 (*)
Ballade No. 2 in F major op. 38 (*)
Nocturne in H major op. 32 No. 1
Piano concerto No. 1 in E minor op. 11 , 2nd movement, Romanza
Prelude in F minor op. 28 No. 18 (*)
Prelude in E-flat minor op. 28 No. 14

Index

A

Abraham 29, 34
Ansermet, E. 88
Augustine, Saint 21

B

Bach, J.S. 7, 68, 79, 97, 140
Balthasar, H.U. von 17, 98
Barth, K. 140
Beethoven, L. van 58, 109, 115, 132
Brahms, J. 97

C

Caravaggio 87, 93
Cloran, E. 107

F

Fontanta, J. 49

G

Gide, A. 7
Gounod, C. 68

H

Heidegger, M. 67
Hillesum, E. 53

I

Ireneus of Lyon, Saint 43
Iwaszkiewicz, J. 128

J

Jesus Christ 43, 73, 77, 78, 100, 121
John, Saint 42, 66, 81

K

Krug, B. 7

L

Luke, Saint 16
Lutosławski, W. 24

M

Mark, Saint 16
Matuszyński, J. 80
Meyer, L. B. 88
Mozart, W.A. 7, 58, 79, 80, 97, 100, 140

N

Natali, L. 82
Newman, J.H. 23
Norwid, C.K. 108, 138

O

Ovid 70

P

Paul, Saint 83
Peter, St 122
Picasso, P. 76
Przybylski, R. 13, 49, 123, 124
Przywara, E. 13

R

Rostworowski, P. 121
Rouault, G. 77

S

Salmann, E. 122
Schubert, F. 97
Schumann, R. 80, 97

W

Wagner, R. 109
Weil, S. 97

Z

Żywny, W. 74

www.ingramcontent.com/pod-product-compliance
Ingram Content Group UK Ltd.
Pitfield, Milton Keynes, MK11 3LW, UK
UKHW041902230426
12049UKWH00002B/9